just in case

1008
Secrets
of a
Happy
Marriage

1008 Secrets of a Happy Marriage

RADIANT SUMMIT BOOKS
Arbuckle, California 1997

RADIANT LIFE SERIES BOOKS:

- • 1008 Secrets of a Happy Marriage
  ISBN: 1–889606–03–0

- • 1008 Secrets of a Happy Marriage
  Gift book newlyweds edition
  ISBN: 1–889606–06–5

Blue Dove Press
P. O. Box 261611
San Diego, CA 92196
telephone (619)-271-0490

Cover and book design:
Poppy Graphics, Santa Barbara, CA

❧ Radiant Life Series:
Inspiring works for inspiring lives

❦

Dedicated to

David & Vita
and
Grace & Chuck

as they begin their journey
up the mountain of love.

 NCE UPON A TIME there was a charming prince named Andrew, who fell in love with a beautiful princess named Cheryl. In the beginning, the two were inseparably in love, but as time wore on, their love slowly began to deteriorate. Petty bickering plagued their relationship as each placed unreasonable demands upon the other.

In a final act of desperation, disillusioned with love, disillusioned with life itself, Princess Cheryl leaped off a high cliff overlooking a tempestuous ocean below. When Prince Andrew heard the news of his beloved's demise, he too, in a final act of anguish, leaped to his death.

When the souls of the prince and princess awoke on the ethereal plane,

they both regretted their foolishness
and their hasty actions.

They vowed, in the future, to come
together and serve as exemplary lovers.
So when the time came for both of
them to experience another round of
birth and death, the pair first requested
an audience with Cupid that they might
be counseled by the master of love, and
by Athena, an angel of wisdom, consid-
ered to be an authority on marriage.

The angel of wisdom was delighted
with the request and agreed to meet
them just three days before Andrew was
to enter his mother's womb to begin his
earthly sojourn. At this meeting, the
pair were tutored by Athena on the sub-
ject of marriage. The prince and
princess were once again reminded of
their past incarnation and the disaster
it had been. To prepare them for their
upcoming birth into new bodies and
eventual marriage together, Athena provided the couple with what amounted to

1008 reminders. She also warned them that all memory of their ethereal meeting would be forgotten on the earthly plane, but the spirit of what had been said would be forever engraved within their hearts.

"You must die to your ego before the wisdom of the heart reveals itself," Athena told them. "The meeting with Wisdom must take place within the heart. The grace of knowledge is always manifested within the heart; it cannot be any other way. And you will always know that it is the grace of wisdom descending upon you because whatsoever comes from the heart will quietly touch every other heart.

"And when the time of your earthly sojourn is nearly over and death draws ever closer, my words will once again be remembered with great passion and intensity. You will be inclined to compile them into a manuscript as a boon to others. You have my blessing to share them with the world. Think of yourself as a pen in Athena's hand.

"But until then, neither of you must ever forget that each of you is born into an earthly existence alone; that each of you is required to find your own happiness and wholeness alone, and that each of you must make the final transition back to an ethereal existence alone. During this allotted time on the earthly plane it will be up to you to make the choice to share your happiness with each other or not. This is what marriage is all about—sharing each other's joyfulness, because this is what each of you are, joy and happiness itself. And how long it takes to realize this is left solely up to you.

"Know that marriage is nothing more than a brief coming together of two souls sharing the lesson of joy with one another. But also know that marriage in and of itself does not automatically guarantee happiness. Joy can only be had by the joyful. Two halfs coming together do not make a whole marriage. It takes two enlightened people to make for a joyful marriage and until the time of enlightenment arrives, there are going to be difficulties to overcome and problems to resolve. This is the challenge of the earthly plane: to regain your lost happiness, to remember you are a being of joy and to share that remembrance with your beloved."

Athena also admonished them that "If you expect your relationship to thrive, you better not be depend on each other to fill those gaps that only your original nature can possibly fill. Know that the first prerequisite to becoming the joyful lover is to be joyfully loving to yourself. If you want to be loved, you must first make yourself lovable. And if you can't love yourself, neither should you expect to be able to love your beloved, neither should you expect to be happy."

The wisdom of Athena was quietly etched in the hearts and souls of the prince and princess. Several days later, Andrew returned to the earthly realm to begin the task of conquering his passions and emotions so that he might master the lessons of marriage.

Neither ever forgot the vow they made in the ethereal realm and as fate would have it, they were brought together in matrimony to be tested as lovers once again. The couple lived out an exemplary life as enlightened lovers, thereby attaining immortality and freeing themselves from what would have been a never-ending round of earthly births and deaths.

During the final days of his life on earth, as the enlightened prince lay on his deathbed, thoughts of his momentous meeting with Athena flooded his mind, just as she had predicted. Filled with inspiration, he dictated these thoughts during the quiet early mornings to his faithful scribe.

The prince then decreed that Athena's wisdom was to be placed on parchment, bound together and distributed free to every couple in the kingdom on their wedding day.

The manuscript became an instant success. After Andrew's death, this tradition was passed on from generation to generation. At every wedding, a copy of this book, *1008 Secrets To A Happy Marriage*, was given as a gift to every bride and groom.

Needless to say, from that point on there were never any divorces or troubled marriages within the kingdom and all the people lived there happily ever after.

And of what Athena taught Prince Andrew and Princess Cheryl prior to their earthly incarnations, this was the sum of her teachings:

1008 Secrets of a Happy Marriage

1. The most overlooked ingredient in a happy marriage is loving yourself, because if you can't love yourself, you can't love someone else.

2. Your number one relationship is with yourself and always will be with yourself; your relationship with your mate reflects how the relationship with yourself is progressing.

3. Marriage only works when both people have their act together; when one or both are immature, there can be much pain and suffering.

4. A rose once a month with love is better than a dozen roses once a year.

5. For communication between two people to be successful, it is necessary to first seek to understand before you can expect to be understood.

6. Two people who love each other can tell each other a thousand things without ever saying a word.

7. Only you know what is best for you and only your mate knows what is best for him or her and to believe otherwise is to court disaster.

8. You can always receive more from your beloved by being in a kind and gentle mood than by being in a demanding one.

9. Never, ever be so preoccupied as to forget the anniversary of your wedding.

10. Laughter is medicine for the soul; if neither of you has laughed today, tickle each other in bed until you do.

11. Marriage should make you light-hearted; if you're married and feel heavy-hearted, you're doing something wrong.

12. A woman's joy is Valentine's Day; a man enjoys Super Bowl Sunday—so cut a deal. Treat her like a queen on her day and treat him like a king on his.

13. Outward beauty promises happiness for male hearts and good looks promise happiness for female hearts, but they are only promises, not guarantees.

14. After fifty years of marriage, don't be surprised if you don't understand each other; you're not supposed to—that would spoil things.

15. Never, ever forget the day your beloved was born.

16. Even if eighty percent of your marriage is going bad and only twenty percent is good, be grateful for that twenty percent.

17. Marital problems cannot be solved as long as someone is being blamed for them.

18. Neither of you is expected to tolerate everything; if you were to tolerate everything you would become a doormat.

19. Household chores should be divided fair and equally, agreeable to both.

20. Too much of a good thing can be wonderful, but remember the pendulum always swings both ways and what is wonderful can become not so wonderful.

21. Don't ever try to hide your unhappiness from the other; you couldn't do it even if you tried, and you just make matters worse.

22. When two people are in love sometimes they don't think; that's the reason for problems, to make us think.

23. Your mate is going to be pleasing at times and annoying at other times; but if you are truly in love, it really shouldn't matter.

24. When you give your beloved something they need more than you need, you give a gift; when you give what you need more than they need, you are gifting them with love.

25. Arguments never determine who is right because everyone has their beliefs to defend; they only determine who speaks louder and is more immature.

26. Every relationship must have boundaries on what we can or cannot do for others and what we can or cannot have done to us.

27. The more important things in life only you can do for yourself.

28. There is nothing impossible for two people in love, as long as both are willing to pay for the consequences of their actions.

29. The final test of love is forgiveness; this is why one must first learn to forgive oneself before forgiving your mate.

30. Reconciliations often require admitting you are wrong when you are wrong, as well as admitting you might be wrong even when you might be right.

31. The only thing you can count on in a marriage is that two people are going to go through a lot of changes together.

32. Sometimes marriage doesn't seem to be worth the effort and then moments later, it all seems worth it and even more.

33. Woe to the household where the rooster crows and the hen runs away or the hen crows and the rooster keeps silent.

34. Avoid couples who place a low value on their marriage; they make marriages ever harder for everyone else.

35. The husband is a conscience for his wife and the wife is a conscience for her husband, and woe to those consciences who do not consult each other periodically.

36. Every man needs to be applauded by his beloved; every woman needs to be complimented by her beloved, both as often as possible.

37. A wise and mature couple will hear each other speak one sentence and understand two.

38. If you want your mate to love you, you must first make yourself lovable.

39. Neither of you should be so preoccupied as to forget the magic words "thank you" and "please."

40. Marriage is not endless bliss and never will be, and to believe so is to set yourself up for disappointment.

41. The successful marriage is all about deciding what your priorities are and then disregarding everything else.

42. There is no such thing as a "normal" marriage; the only normal marriage is between two people who you might think you know, but really don't.

43. Marriages require compromise on an hourly basis.

44. You know you are madly in love when you count the minutes you are apart, but unfortunately, marriage is not about being madly in love.

45. Whenever you laugh together, it takes the kinks out of the invisible chain that binds the two of you together.

46. In a marriage you only get to keep what you give away to your beloved, so give, give, give.

47. There is a criterion by which you can judge whether the things you are doing together are right—have they brought each of you peace and contentment?

48. Don't be bothered by what your beloved says when angry; thick-skinned marriages have a much greater survival rate than thin-skinned ones.

49. You bring just as much suffering into your relationship when you take offense as when you are offensive.

50. If your mate does a mean thing to you, he or she is hurt, not you. You are only hurt if you become embittered or do something back in return.

51. Laughter is always the shortest distance between husband and wife, and anger the longest.

52. There is no way you can get everything you want in a relationship, unless you're a dictator, and then you're going to get even less.

53. It is spontaneous acts of kindness that capture the heart of your mate, not your commands, nor your demands.

54. Life is short so never go through a day without telling your beloved that you love him or her.

55. It's not how many hours you spend with your mate, it's how much of yourself you put into the hours.

56. You cannot not be married on any terms other than equality.

57. Whatever you say in a fit of anger can be forgiven, but it can't be taken back; it can be forgotten, but it can't be recalled.

58. Put your feelings in writing and send your mate a love note whenever the feelings arise.

59. Sometimes marriages require us to make a choice and you have to ask yourself the question: "Do I want half a cookie or none?"

60. Patience and persistence are the most reliable compasses to get two people where they want to go.

61. If the personal boundaries of each other are not respected, the results will be devastating.

62. It takes two people to really argue; one person cannot argue by himself or herself very long.

63. Don't compare your marriage with others; there are some worse, some better. Do the best with what you got.

64. Comunicate your needs as succinctly as possible; don't presume your partner can read your mind, neither of you are mind-readers.

65. If your mate's moods rise and fall like the tides you must learn not only to understand them, but accept and even predict them.

66. Men, as a general rule need to work on giving out more love; women, on not resisting that love when it comes.

67. There's no sense in arguing when you know you're right or arguing when you're wrong; there's no sense in arguing, period!

68. You can always get more from another person by cooperation than you can by stubborn resistance.

69. Talking does not mean you are communicating; what makes communication so difficult is that often the message sent is not the message received.

70. Men don't listen or understand, women talk too much, nag, and complain; these are common marital complaints. Now that you know them, you can do something about them.

71. Never make a decision when you are angry; it will always turn out to be the wrong one.

72. Never go to bed without resolving a dispute, without getting back together again.

73. Trust is the single most important ingredient in the recipe for a successful union of souls.

74. Search for a set of principles to hold your marriage together and then cling to them ferociously.

75. Marriage requires that both people deny themselves in order for it to survive and thrive.

76. Neither of you can resolve the personal problems of another, but you can lend a helping hand along with encouragement.

77. When you care for each other, it shows, and when you don't care, that shows even more.

78. The mate that strives for perfection should strive instead for kindness, because in striving for kindness, you will find perfection.

79. Nothing is more fun than being with someone you want to be with, so tell him or her as often as you can.

80. Quality time is not part-time or divided time; it's full and undivided time.

81. Once a year go to a quiet place and renew your marriage vows with each other.

82. A marriage with short-term and long-term goals, put into writing, is always more successful than marriages that just live from day to day without any goals.

83. Never make a decision that's important without sleeping on it, at least overnight.

84. If two people do not get along in a marriage, it's not a flaw in the institution of marriage, but a flaw in one or both of the individuals in it.

85. Nothing lasts forever; enjoy what you have whenever you have it, as much as you can.

86. You are only given a certain amount of time and to use it to despair, worry, be depressed, feel guilty or to pity yourself is largely a waste of time.

87. The best way to convince your mate to your way of thinking is by being a good example.

88. Enjoy the seasons of life together; never look back with regret at yesterday, always eagerly anticipate tomorrow.

89. The toughest part of marriage is keeping the magic alive after the glitter of being together fades.

90. If your partner does something that hurts you, write him or her a loving letter about your hurts.

91. Forgiveness is not meant for the sake of the forgiven as much as for the sake of the forgiver.

92. Everyone likes to be touched; so give hugs, hold hands, brush against each other, give backrubs, whispers in the ear and kisses galore.

93. Marriage can be like living in heaven, living in hell or living in purgatory; the choice is always up to each of you.

94. Two people can be sleeping under the same roof and one person can be living in heaven and the other in hell.

95. Marriage has been described as licking honey off a thorn; that's because a it's a very delicate undertaking that requires much finesse.

96. What really matters in a marriage is caring for one another; nothing else really matters.

97. Bare hugs are best given in private without any clothes on.

98. Compliments from each other should be accepted graciously, if you want even more compliments.

99. In the beginning was the word and the word was "sex," and it was good.

100. Now that you're married the big questions of life remain yet unanswered: "Who are you? Why are you here?" You can try to answer them together.

101. Avoiding a problem for the sake of keeping peace doesn't make the problem go away, it only makes matters worse.

102. Personal suffering often is the result of not learning to forgive and forget.

103. Never doubt your decision to marry if you want to stay married; there is nothing more insidious than doubt.

104. Marriage becomes intolerable when both of you stop dreaming mighty dreams together.

105. There are storms in every marriage, but the clouds move quickly away and the sun is always there shining.

106. A marriage must have consistency to survive; consistency is what we hold on to when the boat is rocking to and fro.

107. If things get tough and you want your marriage to last, never, ever threaten to leave it—all this creates is emotional blackmail.

108. Treat each other as if each day were your last together; you never know when it just might be.

109. Marriage was designed that we might sing and dance together during joyful times and cry and comfort each other during times of sorrow.

110. Marriage can be either a joyous adventure together or a prison cell built for two; the choice is always yours.

111. Don't confuse the main course in the marriage with dessert; love is the main course, sex is only the dessert.

112. If you continually eat the dessert before the main course, you're going to lose your appetite altogether.

113. There are many marriages lived in quiet desperation, but it need not be that way if you truly love each other.

114. Respect each other's time to be alone; don't assault the privacy of your mate by smothering them with a need for their constant presence.

115. All lovers' quarrels are self-centered and dumb; they arise solely from the ego for the pleasure of the ego.

116. Marriage is not all about wine, good times, and sex; it's all about learning to grow up together.

117. The marriage that ignores the inner life, the spiritual life, is eventually destined for pain and suffering.

118. Always remember that patience is strength in a marriage and without it it is possible to tear down in one hour what it might have taken years to build.

119. Love is what makes all marriages go around; it also makes the ride worthwhile.

120. Marriage is the art of surrendering to each other, and whoever refuses to surrender must live in his or her own self-imposed exile.

121. Don't neglect your solitude; you often must gather your thoughts alone before you can interact with others.

122. Your marriage began as a love affair, and if it is to survive, it must continue to remain a love affair.

123. The courtship of romance does not end at the altar, but it must continue until death if the marriage is to thrive.

124. Marriage is learning the art of not being disappointed by change, and change is the one certainty we can be assured of.

125. Relationships need "prime time" or individual attention in order to flourish.

126. If romance is not kept up in a marriage, it can become a comfortable friendship that is quite "not satisfying."

127. What continued courtship says is "I am not taking this relationship for granted."

128. Don't allow resentments to build up; if you do, they'll become an uncontrollable hornets' nest.

129. Marriage brings with it roles to play—husband and wife, mother and father, and each of us has a different perception how these roles should be acted out.

130. Don't fall into the trap of using "husband" and "wife" as complete job descriptions.

131. You become an expert at marriage only after you learn the worst mistakes you can make and avoid making them.

132. Marriages were not made for one to follow and one to lead, but to walk side by side as partners.

133. A mate is someone who understands where you've been, accepts you for who you are, and extends an invitation to grow together.

134. The only person you can change is yourself and considering how hard it is to change yourself, what chance do you have of changing your mate?

135. Relationships have a magical way of doubling your joys and dividing your sorrows.

136. God gave us two ears and one mouth in order that we might listen twice as much as we speak.

137. Never make a decision when either of you is emotionally upset.

138. The best response to negative words is to say nothing in return, and to negative actions to do nothing; it's a form of "turning the other cheek."

139. Nothing is so fatal to a marriage as indifference; nothing is so beneficial as the enthusiasm of both participants.

140. If you're going to make a mountain out of a molehill, choose the positive aspects to exaggerate in your marriage, not negative ones.

141. Marriage is a gamble—don't allow anyone to tell you otherwise—but only those who dare greatly can achieve greatly.

142. Know that two people must first come together in little things before they can come together in bigger things.

143. A relationship is only as strong as the commitment of each person to the relationship.

144. It's important to know what one wants out of marriage before one is able to get anything out of it.

145. Love is giving without expecting anything in return; that's a very high calling that you both are going to have to grow into slowly.

146. Marriage was designed to share the triumphs as well as the disappointments that occur in everyday living.

147. You will not remember all the days of your marriage; what you will remember are special moments, so make the most of the positive, happy ones.

148. The only marriages that are happy are those where each partner has sought and found how to serve the other.

149. If you give your mate your loving light, whatever darkness there is will disappear of its own accord.

150. When a marriage ceases being an adventure and becomes a convenience, it also becomes something of a trap.

151. Jobs and careers have a way of stressing people and stressed-out people can cause stressed-out marriages.

152. Fantasize together about your tomorrows while enjoying whatever pleasures you may have today.

153. Anger felt but kept quiet leads to resentment, and resentment felt but kept under wraps leads to depression.

154. Love is all or nothing; it is not possible to be loving and angry at the same time, or loving and resentful, or loving and depressed.

155. Sarcasm is a controlled anger that cuts deeper than uncontrolled anger ever could, and besides being uncalled for, is cruel.

156. If you're always putting your mate on the defensive, look close enough and you'll find you're being offensive.

157. All behavior that revolves around the principle, "You hurt me and I am going to hurt you in return," is childish and immature.

158. Sometimes it is better to avoid a conflict and sometimes it is wrong to walk away from one, and common sense is the best indicator.

159. No marriage is ever saddled with a problem without the participants being accorded the strength and stamina to resolve that problem.

160. Admitting you are hurt can be a sign of strength or weakness: strengthening, if it's an actual hurt, weakening, if it is perceived hurt.

161. Perceptions are difficult to unravel in a relationship, because there are so many varied perceptions we have of each other.

162. There are my perceptions of me and your perceptions of you, my perceptions of you and your perceptions of me, and the perceptions we have of each of our perceptions.

163. Never be afraid to tell your mate, "You hurt me and what I need most is for you to love me and care for me, not hurt me."

164. Your attitude about marriage is going to be determined by your attitude about yourself.

165. You can't wait for the "Love Boat" to come to your relationship; you have to swim out to meet it.

166. Marriage should not determine who you are, but help you discover who you are.

167. Every day is a fresh, new experience in your relationship—enjoy it.

168. The easiest person to be is yourself, the hardest person to be is what your mate wants you to be.

169. Children who do not receive warmth and affection are stunted in some way, and the same can be said of our mates.

170. Two hearts that operate on the adage "you can" always have a better happiness rate than one that operates on "you can not."

171. Marriage is the process of helping each other to discover the happiness that dwells within us.

172. Can you imagine what a wonderful relationship everyone would have if each spouse complimented the other instead of complaining about what was wrong?

173. Hugs and kisses shouldn't be a rare treat but a daily occurrence.

174. There will always be those inevitable differences and your happiness depends upon your ability or inability to resolve those differences amicably.

175. If you spend most of your time improving yourself, there will be no time to criticize your other half.

176. You can distinguish real love from unreal love because real love creates and unreal love destroys.

177. If romancing your mate doesn't feel as natural as breathing, you're doing it wrong.

178. There are no two feelings alike and for two people to be alike would not only be unnatural, but quite boring as well.

179. A good healthy relationship needs quality time alone as well as quality time together.

180. The perfect spouse is always too busy for worry, too big for anger, too gentle to hurt, too forgiving to ever be resentful.

181. If you expect only good things from your beloved, more often than not, he or she is going to live up to expectations.

182. It is not your responsibility to make a discontented mate content; only he or she can accomplish that.

183. Always look at the sunny side of your marriage, not the side that is in the shadows.

184. If you talked only happiness, health and prosperity to your other half, there wouldn't be enough time to talk about anything else.

185. Be simple in your desires; there is much more to life than having everything.

186. Generously share your smile; it doesn't cost you a thing and reaps big dividends.

187. Do not expect either praise or reward from your mate for doing things right.

188. Be alert to your spouse's needs if you expect your needs also to be met.

189. Don't be afraid to be spontaneous in your love-making.

190. Take time to smell the flowers together; you'll be glad you did.

191. If you always wait for the perfect time to do something, you'll never get to do anything.

192. When you see rain puddles as a nuisance instead of a plaything, you're losing your sense of humor.

193. Even when your mate seems illogical or unreasonable, love them anyway.

194. The surest way to make your lover trustworthy is to place complete trust in him or her.

195. Save water by taking showers together.

196. Keep a scrapbook, with photos and memorabilia, as a way of celebrating your commitment together, and keep it updated.

197. No one can make you feel inferior unless you grant them permission to do so.

198. Marriages prosper whenever there is a recognition that the participants are creating something important together.

199. Every mate must know and respect the boundaries of the other.

200. It's essential to keep setting aside time to rediscover each other, to remember what brought the two of you together in the first place.

201. Honesty will make you vulnerable, but be honest anyway. It sure beats being dishonest.

202. Don't make the mistake of coming together to make a living instead of coming together to make a life.

203. Marriage doesn't mean you have given up choices; they've just been narrowed down a bit in some ways and expanded in others.

204. Marriage is not a place where we dictate our feelings to another person, but a space where we share our feelings.

205. You can't expect your beloved to bring you total personal fulfillment; to do so would only be asking the impossible from your mate.

206. Whenever you allow the personal problems of your mate to dictate your life, you have become co-dependent.

207. You can only give what you have in your pockets, which means you cannot love your mate unless you first love yourself.

208. The difference between fights in an unhappy marriage and a happy marriage is they they do not spiral out of control in happy ones.

209. Your mate is also your teacher; he or she will teach you how to be and sometimes how not to be.

210. Marriage is like a kerosene lamp; if you want to keep the flame of love lit, you must never stop filling it with oil.

211. A love that turns itself on and off, hot and cold, is an immature love and will suffer from its own mediocrity.

212. It's O.K. to take a break and be alone with yourself when you need it.

213. We do not just suddenly learn how to love. Love requires quality mentors and good teachers are hard to find.

214. Our first glimpse of how love should (or should not) behave came as children when we observed our parents interacting or not interacting together.

215. A daughter observes her mother and learns how to behave as a wife and observes her father and chooses a mate that mirrors an image of him.

216. A son observes his father and learns how to be behave as a husband and observes his mother and chooses a mate that mirrors an image of her.

217. The true cost of a marriage is calculated by the amount of time and effort you are willing to put into it.

218. Surprise your mate every once in a while with breakfast in bed.

219. If you're given a choice between loving and being loved, choose loving because it's much more rewarding giving away love than receiving it.

220. A marriage without enthusiasm is bankrupt; but in a marriage with enthusiasm, the sky's the limit.

221. If your mate has a personal problem and wants you to resolve it, explain lovingly that it's his or her problem and encourage him or her to do so.

222. For a marriage to be a success you have to let go of your mate's personal problems and concentrate on your own.

223. Marriage is a delicate balancing act between giving and receiving and if there is too much of either, the relationship becomes unbalanced.

224. It's O.K. to lovingly say "no" to your beloved without feeling the pangs of guilt later on.

225. Always provide your mate with a golden bridge of forgiveness to retreat over after every confrontation.

226. Holding hands is a sign that romance still exists in your marriage; do it often as possible.

227. Non-sexual touching quietly says, "It's a joy to be near you."

228. Creating a happy relationship is basically simple as long as you continue to remember that what you give to your beloved is exactly what you will receive back.

229. Whenever you love only the best in your lover, you make it easier for that person to love himself or herself even more.

230. If you say "I love you" to a friend, he or she will know exactly what you mean, but lovers can have a difficult time with "I love you," because it means so many different things.

231. There is no word more misunderstood, more misused, than the word "love;" everyone has their own corrupt definition of it.

232. Before you can learn about love, you must first come to an understanding of what love is all about; this can be a difficult, but rewarding undertaking.

233. If you want to learn all about love, you must first learn about those loving qualities that make up a loving person and be loving yourself.

234. One cannot buy the love of another and anyone who believes that love can be bought and sold is deceiving themselves.

235. Place silly love notes as often as possible in unexpected places.

236. Marriage is a commitment to give of oneself without any guarantees expected in return.

237. Share your private thoughts with each other on a regular basis.

238. Marriages thrive only when where there is acceptance by both parties of each other, not continuous complaining.

239. What the commitment of marriage says to your mate is, "I'll be there anytime you might need me."

240. Never be disapproving; what breaks a marriage apart is one mate trying hard to obtain approval and receiving only disapproval.

241. It's the little things you do in a marriage that mean a lot.

242. Give silly little, inexpensive presents to each other for silly little reasons.

243. The question of whether to have children is an issue that both parties should be in complete agreement on.

244. It's dangerous to rely solely upon sex to keep a marriage together and it can be dangerous to deny sex to each other.

245. Have a secret language of "private words" only the both of you understand.

246. Appreciate the specialness of your mate; acknowledge him or her as a one-of-a-kind person, different from everyone else in the world.

247. Never allow the fun of doing things together to be sidetracked by the seemingly more important things that keep you apart.

248. True love doesn't have expectations of being returned; that's what makes it true.

249. When you wound your beloved with unloving words and deeds, apologize immediately and realize it takes time for scars to heal.

250. Make an agreement that during disagreements you'll lower the volume of your voices; there is nothing sillier than an argument in whispers.

251. Marriage has a subtle way of turning two lovers into a dutiful husband and wife if you're not careful.

252. You are only as big as the little things that you let bother you.

253. It's been said that if a mate is upset about something, that makes the problem important.

254. Adult tantrums are no different from children's; if they are not firmly denied, you eventually will be held hostage by them.

255. You are under no obligation to meet a self-centered demand that requires unreasonable attention, except to politely turn it down.

256. Every spouse has an obligation, to themself and to their beloved, to keep themselves fit and healthy.

257. It's how you handle the small nuisances of everyday living that can make or break a marriage.

258. A relationship is all about sharing; if you're doing all the giving and very little receiving, that's not sharing.

259. The successful relationship must learn to give 50-50%; the ideal relationship, 60%-60%.

260. How does one tell a giver from a receiver? A receiver is always making requests and demands, the giver does not know how to make them.

261. Wise couples do not paint themselves into a corner by what they say and then do desperate things to get out of the corner.

262. You can cherish and hold on to your anger and resentment and let it poison you or transmute it into a humbling experience.

263. You transmute your anger and resentment by realizing it is only your stupid, silly, self-centered ego trying to get even with a perceived opponent.

264. Understand that ultimately there are no permanent goals to strive for in a marriage and simply enjoy the ride the two of you are taking together.

265. The self-centered ego thinks in terms of convenience and comfort for the body; it does not think in terms of psychological and spiritual well-being.

266. The self-centered ego sees itself as the center of the universe and acts accordingly; it doesn't deserve any attention.

267. Kindness is a language everyone can easily understand.

268. Whenever you have quarrel with your beloved, the first one who apologizes and says, "I'm sorry, please forgive me," is the winner.

269. Give your mate as much encouragement as you can, but as little of your advice as possible, unless asked for.

270. You have within you the power to make your marriage as joyful or as miserable as you please.

271. If you are dissatisfied with your mate's lovemaking techniques, don't point out his or her failings, but attempt to inform him or her of what your preferences are.

272. It is only when you do not "need" your beloved that your relationship with him or her can become whole and complete.

273. Love teaches us to show our feelings, but love can only show positive feelings; love would never think of bothering its beloved with negative feelings.

274. Don't try to be in control; the penalty for the manipulation of the people you care for the most is the feeling that you are not being loved in return.

275. True love can only be really understood by the giver, seldom by the receiver. Why is this so? Because love is all about giving, not receiving.

276. Angry spouses need help, not condemnation; they pay a heavy price indeed for their indiscretions.

277. Marriage is like a flower: if it's not watered, weeded and fed, it won't bloom, and if left untended will wither and die.

278. Love is flowing with the river, not paddling against it; it's accepting your mate for who they are, not who you want them to be.

279. To live in gratitude to your mate is to live a life of abundance even if you have nothing else.

280. Love doesn't look back, love doesn't regret yesterday, nor is it anxious about tomorrow; love is always taking place now in the present moment.

281. Send your mate a fax announcing how much you love them.

282. It is not differences that tear a marriage apart, but the escalating conflict and divisiveness that some differences bring about.

283. The bottom line of marriage is that a husband and wife have no choice but to love one another; it's either that or live in the absence of love, which is hell.

284. To be loving is often to be misunderstood; there are few people able to understand the subtle nuances of love, but after several decades you might realize them.

285. One does not learn to be a good husband or a good wife in a class or from a book; one learns that role only by trial and error.

286. Marriage offers an endless array of joy if that is what you are looking for or endless misery if that is what you are looking for, the choice is always yours.

287. Only two kinds of people are truly able to love: an innocent child and an enlightened adult, so until you become enlightened, hang in there.

288. Love cannot be weighed nor can it be measured; it can only be felt by loving and sometimes by receiving, but mostly by giving.

289. Love never feels lonely because love can never be lonely; it is too busy loving.

290. If you look for the very best in your mate, you'll always find it, and you'll find the worst if you look hard enough for that too.

291. If you offer your mate love and it is refused, there is no need to despair; he or she is just not yet ready to be loved.

292. Love is a force, even as hate, evil and anger are forces, except that love is a greater force.

293. If you find love lacking in your relationship, you only have yourself to blame.

294. A relationship is like every other experience of life: you only get out of it what you are willing to put into it.

295. When needs are not met, anger and resentment generally result; this is why self-reliance is so important within a relationship—it reduces needs by making one content with very little.

296. Try to give your mate a compliment about their cooking after every meal.

297. Love has no inclination to lead, or to follow, or to control; its only interest is in finding a way to share.

298. Be content with what you have; more comfort and convenience in a marriage does not bring with it any more happiness or a better chance for survival; often it causes even more friction.

299. Love is only love when it helps you discover what you have been searching for since time immemorial—your Self.

300. One person's contentment can be another's boredom and dissatisfaction, and this is where compromise plays an important role in your marriage.

301. Always try to look ahead; there shouldn't be a need to look back on a former relationship except as an experience to learn from.

302. The search for love within a marriage is really the search for God, for God is love and marriage is the means by which you learn to love.

303. Be adventuresome; beware of falling into the rut of routine—the old, familar ways are more comfortable than the new and untried, but never as rewarding.

304. Marriages require work to keep them going; it's not just doing nothing wrong—it also requires doing many things right.

305. Having children is not the cure-all for marital problems, but often makes the problems between two people even worse.

306. In a healthy relationship, you can't touch each other too much and unhealthy ones are known for their lack of touchng.

307. Self-esteem is a prerequisite of a happy marriage because only when you are feeling good about yourself are you able to feel good about your spouse.

308. When your mate is angry or sullen, he or she is hurting himself or herself more than you.

309. It has been argued that sharing your emotions is what love is all about— but this is only half the truth, because love does not know how to share negative emotions.

310. Love is all about sharing positive emotions, not negative ones; what lover would want to share rage, jealousy, envy, and despair with their beloved?

311. As you learn to love yourself, your relationship changes; it may be a little or a lot or completely, but your relationship changes.

312. No matter how great your love for your mate, it's just not possible to be everything to him or her.

313. Make it a rule to do something together (only the two of you) at least once a week.

314. Both of you must learn that you are opposite sexes, but not necessarily opposing sexes.

315. The purpose of marriage is not to be successful, but loving; when you are loving, your marriage cannot help but be successful. This does not mean your efforts will play out in the way you expect.

316. Men make women feel desirable and feminine; women make men feel desirable and masculine—such is the merry-go-round of sex, so enjoy the ride with each other.

317. If you have low self-esteem, a poor relationship with yourself, you are going to have a poor relationship with your beloved also.

318. Your health is your wealth; treat your body well and it will treat you well; without a healthy body it is difficult to have a healthy relationship.

319. The mate who is more loving will always be taken advantage of by the other because the loving mate never has demands to be met, and not being demanding always makes for a happier marriage.

320. You deserve love and respect and kindness from your significant other just because you're you and for no other reason.

321. Whenever you throw mud at your mate, you end up with dirty hands yourself.

322. Even the most stable marriages go through periods of dissatisfaction; that's why it's important not to say or do anything that you might regret later.

323. Even catchy phrases like "I love you" are just words when they fail to come from the heart.

324. A mate that has a tendency to be angry is wrong even when they are right.

325. Being of good cheer and humor, joking around, silliness and playful teasing are all ways to create a positive energy within a marriage.

326. Curiosity, wonder and enthusiasm are what make children so alive; they also are the essential ingredients that keep a relationship alive and together.

327. Don't ever talk about your mate behind his or her back; he or she will somehow sense the discordant vibrations.

328. Don't make comparisons of your present relationship with other relationships unless you are looking to create a lot of trouble for yourself.

329. Marriages fail because of unfulfilled expectations, so the fewer expectations you have, the better the chances for survival.

330. Judgments focus on tearing relationships apart by separation; forgiveness, on bringing people together through wholeness.

331. A good sex life does not insure compatibility between two people; although it may help, it is not the end all in itself.

332. Marriages are all about two beginners learning how to be experts in a relationship through trial and error.

333. How can you tell if your marriage is going well? If your mate is moody, angry or complaining, it ain't; if he or she is smiling and happy, it is.

334. Love is the most misunderstood word in the world, and for most people it is confused with sex, but sex is not love nor is love sex.

335. Being a success at work is not worth it if it also means being a failure at home.

336. Try to keep your life spontaneous because what provokes spontaneous behavior in a marriage is beneficial to that marriage, what dampens it, is harmful.

337. Everyone is required to learn the lesson of forgiveness and marriage is an ongoing classroom to teach you how to be forgiving.

338. Whenever you allow burdensome duties and responsibilities to dominate your life, you relinquish your responsibility to yourself to be happy and your marriage suffers as a result.

339. Admit your mistakes. There's nothing to be ashamed of in making a mistake—just in repeating the mistake over and over again.

340. Listening is always the best bridge between husband and wife; a wise mate is always a neutral listener.

341. The phrases "you should" and "you shouldn't" only reveal a rigidity on the part of the person who uses them and are not acceptable in a marriage of equality.

342. What commitment does is give two people the courage to endure while they are sanding down the rough edges of each other's ego.

343. Love is always accepting; it does not try to remake the object of its affection in its own image.

344. Praise of your mate is free, but it always finds a way to pay one back.

345. Self-esteem is not pride, nor should it be confused with the ego; self esteem is loving oneself without pride and that is a godlike quality.

346. Manipulation and control by one mate of another seldom works because most people naturally resist being controlled.

347. When you make judgment of your mate, you are also making judgment of your own self, you are making judgment of your own superiority or inferiority.

348. If you want to be loved more than you are, sometimes you have to make yourself worth loving even more.

349. It's not necessary to have the last word; sometimes having the last word is the first step to yet another argument.

350. Men are generally attracted to women for what they are; and women are generally attracted to men for what they might be.

351. Great lovers do not just happen; they consciously take the quality time it requires to become great lovers.

352. A happy relationship can be measured by how comfortable you feel in your beloved's presence; the less comfortable the feeling, the less happiness there is.

353. Never doubt your decision to marry; once you begin seriously questioning, "Should I have married or not?" you probably shouldn't have.

354. The ego is not you. The ego is a mask, a false personality. You can wear many masks, but they are always false because you are Love Itself and Love does not wear a mask.

355. The worst thing you can do for a relationship is to burden your mate with impossible expectations that he or she is unable to meet.

356. Marriage is an adventure into the unknown, designed for you to get to know yourself, and until that happens, every marriage will find something lacking, and naturally so.

357. Marriage is not for one who bores easily because it requires keeping your undivided attention upon your mate for a very long time.

358. If a marriage is to be a success, it's not about finding Mister or Ms Right, but by _being_ Mister or Ms Right.

359. Neither man nor woman comes to the altar of marriage without need for further personal growth and that is what relationships are all about—enhancing personal growth.

360. When couples are courting, they continually think of things to please one another; this practice should not stop simply because you get married.

361. Marriage vows do not make two imperfect people into a perfect couple, but actually can accentuate problems. But this can be a great blessing because we grow through solving our problems.

362. Any lover can tell you that if you have to ask yourself the question, "How do I know I am in love?" you're usually not in it.

363. Marriage, if practiced correctly, should encourage each of you to put away childish behaviors and grow up.

364. If you try to make your mate into someone who he or she was never meant to be, you are not only wasting your time, but theirs as well.

365. A successful marriage is often best achieved by keeping your heart open and your mouth closed.

366. Make up a list of the things you like about your mate and, after framing it, make a point to read it everyday.

367. Learn a thousand and one ways to tell your mate how wonderful he or she is.

368. Marriages were not made to be critical of each other, but to compliment each other.

369. Share each other's happiest moments of the day every evening.

370. Every marriage begins with great potential, but that potential cannot be realized without sacrifice and hard work.

371. If your mate has something important to say, yield without interruption.

372. Marriage doesn't always give you what you want, but it does have a way of giving you what you need when you need it.

373. The successful marriage is all about enriching each other without impoverishing yourself.

374. No mate is obligated to honor all the requests made by a significant other, only to honestly consider them.

375. If each of you doesn't try to bring out the best in the other, who else is going to?

376. Marriage has a way of changing perspectives, so make sure you don't allow the things that brought you together to die from neglect.

377. Whatever it is you earnestly look for in your mate is what you will eventually find, good or bad.

378. When you joke at your mate's expense, it's rude, but also not very funny.

379. Don't discuss any emotionally charged issues until both of your emotions have sufficiently quieted down.

380. If you love your mate with the expectation of getting something back in return, sometimes you're going to be disappointed.

381. It's always easier to change a "no" to a "yes" than to change a "yes" to a "no."

382. Arguments should be instruments to clear up misunderstandings, not to battle one another about who is right and who is wrong.

383. Whoever masters his or her tongue in a relationship not only has mastery over himself or herself but the relationship as well.

384. A successful marriage is like playing the piano: unless you practice daily you're going to be off-key sometimes.

385. Never argue in public; always clean your dirty laundry in private.

386. When you negotiate with your spouse, don't be afraid to put all your cards on the table; only by doing so, will you be able to arrive at a mutually acceptable solution.

387. Make your marriage an adventure; whenever you have a choice among several things, try the one you've never tried before.

388. It is not what you say to your mate that matters as much as the tone of voice you say it in.

389. Marriage is probably the most important decision you'll ever make because it determines who you are going to spend the rest of your life with.

390. The participants in a healthy marriage soon learn it is necessary never to forget some things and never to remember others.

391. Apologies are the quickest way to make a wrong a right.

392. Love is not blind, although it pretends at times to be blind; it is passion that is blind.

393. Whenever you make judgment of your beloved, what you are generally doing is adding qualities that are not there and leaving out qualities that make him or her unique.

394. It is immature for one mate to put the other under a magnifying glass with constant suggestions how to change.

395. Marriage should be the art of making the most of what you've got and the least of what you don't have.

396. There is always something more important in a relationship than your own selfishness.

397. Never fail to give appreciation for the littlest of things your beloved does for you.

398. A mate that is committed to a marriage can give one hundred reasons to stay in one; a mate that is not, a hundred reasons why not to.

399. A part of romance is having a romantic setting when you make love: this means soft lights, music, fragrances, silk sheets, and alluring clothing.

400. A love that focuses exclusively on one person to the exclusion of everyone else is an unbalanced affair waiting to fall apart.

401. "Nagging" is a common marital practice that only makes matters worse.

402. When a woman wants a "knight in shining armor," what she is looking for is a man whom she can admire.

403. People marry because they have a need to be admired, stimulated, cared for and nurtured by another person, so do it!

404. When you surprise your mate with a small gift or flowers, make it a meaningful gesture and not an obligation.

405. Never, ever forget your mate on Valentine's Day if you want to remain together as lovers.

406. There are no shortcuts to a successful marriage; each of you must walk every step of the way together.

407. To stop pushing, to cease controlling, to let things happen, to surrender to your marriage takes enormous courage, but is well worth the effort.

408. Be persistent in your loving each other as water is persistent; when water meets an obstacle, it stops, stores up and either pushes the obstacle away or flows around it.

409. Whenever you discover goodness in your mate, imitate it; and if you discover anything other than goodness, accept it.

410. Slow growth in a marriage is good, it forms deep, thick roots; fast growth, shallow and spindly ones that are uprooted at the slightest storm.

411. It is only by piling up many little rocks over a period of time that we create an immovable mountain of stability.

412. The three most important words in a marriage are not necessarily "I love you," but "I'm sorry dear," or "please forgive me."

413. Feelings of inferiority only serve to prove you haven't learned to love yourself enough yet.

414. For self-esteem to be valid, it must be stronger than anyone else's rejection of you.

415. Self-esteem is the element that gives each person the wherewithal to meet the challenges of marriage; without self-esteem there cannot be a happy marriage.

416. Share your duties; if you hold the belief that if you want the job done right you're going to have to do it yourself— you certainly haven't learned the lesson of sharing.

417. If both players in a marriage cannot be true to themselves, the whole marriage is false and waiting to fall apart.

418. Two people who care for and love each other unconditionally is an example of practical spirituality at its very best.

419. There is only one reality in a relationship and that is for the heart to do what it loves doing best.

420. All relationships have their limitations, like the banks of a river, but understand that without the banks, there would be no river.

421. It's O.K. for you to make plans for your marriage as long as you don't always expect your plans to happen in a certain way; life just doesn't work that way.

422. The inferior mate is offended by imperfection and is always making his or her criticisms known; the superior mate is quietly accepting, without ever being offended.

423. There are always two ways to fail in a relationship—by trying too little and by trying too much.

424. The fewer expectations you have, the more likely they will manifest, because the moment one gives up all expectations, the universe rushes in to fill the void.

425. When you give up striving and live life with contentment, even little achievements can bring great fulfillment.

426. If something in your marriage no longer works for you, don't look at it as a failure, but as a completion; move on to something else.

427. Your worthiness and your mate's worthiness have nothing to do with personal achievement; both of you are worthy simply because of who you are.

428. The secret to good communication is to replace all judgment with simple observation; to replace all faultfinding with acceptance.

429. If you're always saying to yourself "I'll be happy when...," you'll never get around to enjoying what you have now.

430. You are never obligated to meet your mate's emotional demands; you may do so, but it is not your duty to meet demands. Why is this so? Because true love is never demanding!

431. Marriage doesn't resolve pre-existing problems. The problems you had before marriage will only surface more quickly afterwards.

432. Your partner does not have the magical power to lift you out of the blues; that power lies within your own personal domain—the doorway to happiness is unlatched from within.

433. A co-dependency is the result of two people relying upon each other for their happiness instead of sharing their happiness together.

434. Marriage is the weaving together of two strands of soul until they are so intricately woven together, they cannot be taken apart or both will be damaged in the process.

435. A relationship is always enhanced when you are able to fulfill your needs without making demands upon your beloved in the process.

436. Marriage can be more demanding and harder than being single; it can also be more rewarding and challenging.

437. The bird has a nest, the spider its web, and men and women their homes. Treat yours as you would a sacred sanctuary; it is your refuge from the world.

438. The reality of intimacy is not always as exciting as fantasies of intimacy.

439. Many couples go into marriage thinking it's a pot of gold; well, it's a pot of gold alright, but only after being purified by the fire of difficulties.

440. The most sensible plan for making a marriage work is not to demand perfection and to be able to accept imperfection without complaining.

441. Self-esteem is accepting who we are complete with our inadequacies and misunderstandings of who we are.

442. Your first love affair should be with yourself; after you have been successful loving yourself, you can go on and share that love with your beloved.

443. Inward and outward stress both have a way of dampening sexual desire if allowed to run rampant.

444. The secret to a happy marriage is keeping the original magic alive, and how is this done? That's a secret you both have to discover for yourselves.

445. The surrender of personal principles should in no way ever be a part of compromise with your beloved.

446. When couples respond to each other as best friends, there is generally more harmony because as best friends there is less need to behave in a certain way.

447. What marriage is all about is a lot of compromise and if you can't compromise, perhaps you shouldn't be married.

448. Relationships are not a game where both sides "keep score."

449. Marriage works best when you believe your mate's happiness is just as important as your happiness.

450. There is nothing that sabotages a relationship more than doubt about the relationship itself.

451. Don't play games with each other's minds; when one mate attempts to manipulate another, to dominate another, it degrades the entire relationship.

452. There should be nothing out of bounds in your sex life as long as it is enjoyable to the both of you and it does not hurt anyone.

453. Innocence believes marriages are made in heaven, but experience knows better, realizing that heaven and hell are both states of mind.

454. People who unconditionally love themselves find it easy to surrender to their beloved without making demands.

455. Threatening to leave a relationship has a way of undermining it even more.

456. Marriage is not for the immature who don't have the slightest idea who they are; two immature people equals one troubled marriage!

457. Relationships are for enhancing your identity, not losing it; if you lose your identity in a marriage, you're doing it all wrong.

458. Surrender is an essential ingredient to love because without surrender to one's beloved, love can never be complete.

459. The job of each of you is to act as helpmate to the other, not to behave like a parent; to play the role of partner, not the role of a boss.

460. There is no place for anger in a relationship; anger closes the door to reconciliation and makes the other person defensive, while praise opens one up to being more receptive.

461. Don't judge your partner by what he or she will do or not do for you.

462. Never tell your mate, "I know exactly how you feel," because the odds are you don't and never will be able to.

463. Marriage is not all bliss, but has a way of accentuating the highs and lows of life; so be prepared for both.

464. Never sink to the level of your beloved, but always be ready to rise to his or her level if need be.

465. Talking out things with your mate sometimes requires more intimacy between two souls than just lovemaking.

466. A steady diet of anger will wear away the fabric of every relationship.

467. What makes anger so devastating is that it foolishly tries to destroy one person's ego by building up another.

468. The best way to be happy in a relationship is to determine what would make your beloved happy and then encourage him or her to do it.

469. If communication in a marriage is not being done lovingly, it should not be done at all.

470. It's not what a marriage has that makes you happy, or what you do in the marriage, but who you are in the marriage.

471. Relationships become difficult when people change and never get around to telling each other.

472. When your mate becomes overly possessive, it sometimes becomes necessary to assert your rights in a loving way.

473. You are never under any obligation to accept anything other than love and kindness from your mate.

474. Once you begin to take your marriage for granted, you lose the spark that ignited it in the first place.

475. A perfect lover is also an unconditional lover. There is absolutely no difference between the two.

476. Compromise is what makes a marriage work with one exception: when you compromise character values.

477. No husband has property rights on his wife, no wife has property rights on her husband. There are no exceptions.

478. Don't be afraid to waste time just being together; life is more than spinning your wheels trying to get from point A to point B.

479. Every relationship is built on a delicate balance, and that balance cannot be defined because it's like riding a bicycle built for two.

480. One of the main reasons two people come together is to find security in an unsecure world.

481. Don't say yes when you want to say no and don't say no when you want to say yes.

482. If your happiness depends upon your mate, he or she holds all the power in the relationship, and neither of you is going to be happy.

483. It's O.K. to set boundaries on what is acceptable and unacceptable in your relationship, as well as the repercussions if the boundaries are crossed.

484. You are accountable for your happiness and your mate is accountable for his or her happiness; you can share your happiness but you can't give it to each other.

485. Keep your word; broken promises betray your lack of trust.

486. Commitment is not only an important ingredient in marriage; it's an essential element in every successful venture of life.

487. By understanding the uniqueness of your mate, you allow them to be who they are and you grow too.

488. There is quite a difference between needing things from your mate and demanding them and a healthy marriage will have few needs and no demands because all needs will be naturally met.

489. When a need becomes a want, it suddenly becomes a necessity and when a necessity becomes a demand, a relationship becomes unbalanced.

490. There is nothing like a good sense of humor to keep spirits up and put things in their proper perspective.

491. Be consistent; if you're not consistent in your actions with your mate, you're going to subconsciously pin a label on yourself called "inconsistent."

492. It's O.K. to make a decision not to make a decision, but it's not O.K. to make a decision strictly by default or because you're afraid to.

493. A relationship helps us to broaden our viewpoint by seeing things from a wider perspective, with four eyes instead of two.

494. Don't make the mistake of defending your old, bad habits just because it's easier not to make a change.

495. The most difficult honesty is with yourself and if you're not honest with yourself, how are you going to be honest with your mate?

496. Try to put yourself in your mate's place and you'll be following the Golden Rule, "Do unto others as you would have them do unto you."

497. You learn to discover and control your feelings and emotions by talking them out with your mate, not by acting them out.

498. There are no lousy duties in a marriage, only lousy attitudes.

499. Your needs control you and sometimes your wants and desires control you, but when you control your needs, wants, and desires, they become choices.

500. There are no magical solutions for marital problems with one exception— prevention of the problem; the successful marriage is one that heads off problems before they become troublesome.

501. Sexual intimacy does not guarantee heart-to-heart intimacy; this is only achieved when two people have gotten rid of their egos.

502. Everyone knows what's right in a relationship, the hard part is subduing the ego enough to put it into practice.

503. Giving, not receiving is the secret to practicing unconditional love and partaking of its mysterious joy.

504. Love never makes demands upon another person and a love that does demand is not really love nor will it ever be.

505. Conflict is most easily avoided when both parties assume a win-win attitude.

506. When you learn to truly like yourself, you'll laugh at yourself for once trying to be like others.

507. The test of your commitment in a marriage is not how you act when things are going good, but how you act when things are not going so good.

508. Everyone has 168 hours each week to do whatever it is he or she wants to do. Part of that time should be devoted to your mate and part to yourself.

509. A healthy relationship is loving your mate for who they are today not for who they might be tomorrow or who they were yesterday.

510. It's O.K. to have your needs met first as long as you don't hurt your beloved in the process.

511. There are two choices in life: being a phony, someone other than who you really are, or just being yourself; in every successful marriage both participants are just being themselves.

512. Don't be a perfectionist; that's someone who flip-flops back and forth from being perfect to being worthless and never finds a happy medium.

513. Never regret what happened yesterday, nor be apprehensive about tomorrow.

514. Learn to be patient with your mate; when you let impatience get the best of you, you want what you want and you want it now and that always is a prescription for trouble.

515. The compulsion to be perfect not only hurts you, but disturbs the equilibrium of those who are closest and dearest to you as well.

516. No marriage begins as a permanent success; to make it successful you must keep on keeping on.

517. Successful marriages are not handed to people on a silver platter; they require work, lots of hard work.

518. Patience and persistence are valuable allies in a marriage; your enemy is always impatience and giving up.

519. Everyone must assume 100 percent responsibility for his or her choices and to blame someone else for choices you have made is simply a matter of immaturity.

520. If you want your communication with your mate to be effective, look eye to eye when you are communicating with him or her.

521. When you plant a seedling, you don't expect it to grow into a giant tree overnight; well, the same can be said of marriages.

522. All choices have their rewards or consequences, depending upon your motives; therefore the key to every marital choice is simply: "What is your motive?"

523. The successful marriage is one with a maximum of life and a minimum of strife.

524. Never point a finger of blame at your mate when things aren't going well with you—that's a cop-out!

525. Don't be afraid to take risks together. The marriage that takes no risks never gets to test its true potential.

526. Use your mistakes as opportunities to learn together, not as a means to getting down on each other.

527. Take time to spend the entire day together every once in a while doing whatever it is you both love to do most.

528. Use successful marriages of people you know as a role model for your relationship.

529. Don't be reluctant to walk the more difficult path together. Choosing the path of least resistance creates even more weakness, certainly not strength.

530. Establish short time limits for any marital disagreements and keep to them.

531. Marriage is a full-time job; learn to say "no" to activities that are a waste of each other's time.

532. Successful role models for your marriage are not just to be admired, but queried, listened to and their advice diligently followed.

533. It's O.K. for two people to disagree. What's not O.K. is to be disagreeable during the disagreement.

534. Find a mentor with a proven marital track record and use him or her as a sounding board when difficulties arise.

535. There cannot be any growth in a dependent relationship until the dependency is broken in a loving way.

536. Don't try to buy your beloved's affection; what this means is don't spend large amounts of money on things you can't afford just to please each other.

537. You cannot be partially committed to a marriage and expect complete satisfaction; it's an all or nothing thing.

538. It doesn't matter what the commitment is; if a person is not committed 100 percent, he or she is not really committed at all.

539. You both know you and your mate are different; the challenge is for you to find out how much you are alike.

540. Commitment requires acceptance of the faults and limitations of your mate and learning to make the best of them.

541. Every person must do their own growing; no one can do your growing for you, not even your own mate.

542. The essential ingredient that glues every marriage together is "caring."

543. Whenever you or your mate changes, so does the dynamic within the marriage, which means you can expect your marriage to be continually changing.

544. The difference between partial commitment and total commitment is the difference between success and failure of a marriage.

545. If you look at everything that happens in your marriage as the best thing that could have happened, it will be so.

546. Make changes slowly; a dramatic change in you can often trigger fear in your mate when they are too insecure to change on their own.

547. No one can control all the circumstances in their relationship, but you can control your response to every circumstance.

548. A change in you can often inspire a similar change in your mate; example is always the most efficient teacher.

549. A marriage that is measured in terms of material possessions is using a false criterion for success.

550. By first caring for your personal needs you learn how to realize your mate's needs.

551. Don't shirk problems. Often a crisis is just what is needed to bring unknown strengths into a marriage.

552. Give a little more than you receive during every marital transaction; the reward will be beyond measure.

553. Listening is the best way to catch your mate's attention; understanding is the quickest way to catch his or her heart.

554. Some of your more important conversations are the ones straightening out yourself, not your mate.

555. When you put yourself completely in the hands of another person, you have lost control of your identity.

556. Only by learning how to politely say "no" to others can you gain enough time to do those things you want to do with your beloved.

557. Don't ever blame your mate for your unhappiness; it is you who makes the choice whether to be cheerful or gloomy—not your partner.

558. Respect is the oil that lubricates a marriage and keeps it running smoothly during the most difficult times.

559. When accurate communication does not take place, it leaves room for guessing and generally such guessing tends to be negative.

560. You have no right to expect either yourself or your mate to be a mind reader; that is why communication is so vitally important.

561. Dialogue is always helpful as long as it is not blaming, insulting, criticizing, demanding or judgmental.

562. Whenever you say, "Nothing is bothering me" when something is, you're not only being dishonest to your mate, but to yourself as well.

563. When communicating, try to avoid absolute phrases like "you never" and "you always."

564. Long-lived relationships maintain that "respect" is the number-one ingredient in a successful union of two hearts.

565. Association with optimistic couples makes it easier for your marriage to remain optimistic.

566. Marital maturity is understanding that the greatest pleasures in life are relatively free, requiring nothing more than a payment of gratitude.

567. Any bad habit that has been learned is a habit that can be unlearned if you are earnest enough in overcoming it.

568. Relationships never really improve until the individuals within them have improved themselves.

569. With your negative thoughts you can quietly push your mate away and with your positive thoughts you can bring him or her even closer.

570. Always try to have a positive slant on things and keep your mind open to the other point of view, especially when it is divergent.

571. Nagging does not make a spouse more teachable; it builds barriers even higher because it results in one person's tuning the other person out.

572. A good balanced relationship is one that does not require someone else to make you happy.

573. Anger is a need for power expressed; it's just another way of saying "If you don't do as I say, I'm going to punish you in one way or another."

574. Personal change can begin whenever, however and wherever you want to begin—if you want it badly enough!

575. Whenever you turn your personal power over to your mate, you are abdicating responsibility for yourself.

576. The more you give up in order to be loved by your spouse, the less you end up loving yourself.

577. "Thank you" and "please" are signs of appreciation and respect between two people.

578. It's nice to share your thoughts and ideas with your mate as long as you're not doing it to brag or seek approval.

579. The quickest way to influence your mate is by being sincerely complimentary.

580. Marriages bond together through similar tastes and grow stronger through differences.

581. Whenever you have something important to say to your mate, do it with level eye contact at arm's length away.

582. You are not your relationship, you are your consciousness, and should your relationship die, you do not die, unless you allow yourself to.

583. Without joy there is no love, and love without joy is a false love.

584. It is by giving that one receives in a marriage; it is by forgetting oneself that one finds oneself.

585. People do not learn to grow in the shadow of another; everyone must grow by casting their own shadow. This is why a certain amount of space is required between two people who are growing.

586. Watch your words—the same word can have two completely different meanings to two different people and cause great misunderstanding.

587. You can't ask yourself, "Am I getting all the happiness I can get from my marriage?" until you first ask yourself, "Am I giving all the happiness I can give?"

588. When you "grow up" you will find out that the immature heart is continually finding ways to shed tears of sorrow; the mature heart, tears of joy.

589. The calmness of one heart during a dispute sometimes has a strange way of setting off fury in another heart; but this should not dissuade you from remaining peaceful.

590. Don't ever ask your mate if he or she loves you, because it only serves to imply that you have failed to perceive it.

591. The things that count most in a marriage are the little things that cannot be qualified by words or quantified by numbers.

592. As long as your self-esteem depends upon what someone else says about you, there can be little personal satisfaction.

593. Keep in touch with each other's feelings; it's a mistake to believe what feels good for you automatically feels good to your lover.

594. Trust your heart not your mind; problems are solved best by the loving heart, and made worse by solutions reached by the logical mind.

595. The only permanence in marriage is the commitment itself; everything else about relationships is in a continual state of change.

596. Never be afraid to give your all to your beloved. In the language of hearts there are never any mistakes, only learning experiences.

597. Human failure results from the lack of love; but as long as one remains loving, one can never be a failure.

598. It is foolishness to think that we can shape our lives, when all the time life is shaping us.

599. If a relationship is to succeed, both hearts must spend more time in contemplation and less time in speculation.

600. In a marriage, suffering can never result for a heart that seeks nothing but to give freely of itself.

601. The crowning glory of marriage is two people growing old together in an atmosphere of immense peace and love.

602. "Communication" does not mean you have to agree with your mate; it just requires politely considering his or her point of view without prior judgment.

603. It is the unhappy heart that fears change; the happy heart looks forward to change and so does a successful union of two hearts.

604. Problems within a relationship must always be dealt with on the level of cause, not by tinkering with effects.

605. To make a marriage work, both partners must accept the whole package, not just bits and pieces of it.

606. Love is the divine ideal and marriage is everyday reality, and and the wise couple never gets the two mixed up.

607. Trust is only a partial ingredient in a relationship; being worthy of that trust is what completes it.

608. It's O.K. to make plans regarding your relationship as long as you don't plan the results—that's in higher hands.

609. Most of the time your mate is willing to meet the expectations you have of him or her; this is true in a positive way as well as a negative one.

610. Be yourself; when you try to make an impression on your mate, what you are doing is only giving the impression you're trying to make an impression.

611. Relationships have a funny way of teaching us humility, and if we aren't humble enough, they will soon do everything possible to humble us.

612. When you turn your relationship over to God, God will send just the problems both of you need in order to grow.

613. You gain respect when you admit you're wrong and lose respect when you accuse your mate of being wrong.

614. The greatest problem in a relationship is you; you are your own problem, along with your errant way of thinking.

615. It's much easier looking ahead into the future than to regret the past, but every relationship must eventually learn to live in the here and now and not be tied down by either the past or the future.

616. You can travel halfway around the world and the problems encountered by two people in a relationship will change little.

617. Marriage often ends up like a game of cards: you have to play the game the best you can, with the cards you have.

618. If a relationship is not in the process of growing and improving, it's deteriorating.

619. Being a good example is preferable to preaching to someone else to be a good example.

620. Every time you set conditions on how your mate should behave, you take away his or her freedom as well as yours.

621. It is not your responsibility to make your mate happy, it's his or her obligation; you can only give him or her encouragement and support.

622. Your happiness depends upon you, not your beloved; when you believe otherwise, you both have a problem.

623. Acceptance is focusing on your mate's positive attributes, not on his or her negative ones.

624. If there is something about your mate that irritates you, that's your problem, not his or hers.

625. Immature love has a way of laying a guilt trip by saying, "I'm unhappy, I'm living in hell, and you're to blame."

626. Loving your mate doesn't mean that just because he or she is miserable, you are required to be miserable too.

627. The fruit of a relationship is not within arm's distance; it requires that each person climb out on a limb to get it.

628. True love would never say, "If you really love me, you'll do as I say"; that's just the ego speaking.

629. Reforming your mate is like reforming the world; it's frustrating work and seldom worth the effort.

630. The healthy relationship is the one that allows the other person to change his or her mind without getting upset by it.

631. When you give your mate a present, it's not cool to expect one in return.

632. Accepting your beloved's beliefs does not mean you have to invalidate your own beliefs.

633. Communication gets derailed whenever there is either a need to be right or a need to prove someone wrong.

634. Relationships are difficult because people are complex; what might work for one couple can be a total disaster for another.

635. The more time you spend analyzing a relationship, the less time you have to live it.

636. The depth of one's character reveals itself best in times of adversity.

637. The giver in a relationship always gets back more than the receiver, because for the giver the giving is reward enough.

638. Don't make the mistake of assuming you know your mate; you may be surprised to find out you didn't know him or her as well as you thought.

639. Half the problems in a relationship would vanish overnight if people only stopped getting upset over what their mates said or did to them.

640. Relationships begin cracking at the seams whenever demands are placed upon them that cannot be satisfied.

641. Relationships are not meant to go backwards, they must travel forward or not at all.

642. Growing up in a relationship is all about what the common vernacular calls "getting your shit together."

643. The bottom line of every marriage: each person wants to be understood, accepted and appreciated.

644. All growth within a relationship requires change and change often requires abandonment of what we are presently accustomed to having.

645. Sometimes you can't help a mate who refuses to face his or her addiction to drugs, alcohol, gambling or food. However, your unconditional love may provide the space for them to change.

646. If you want something from your mate and can't get it, there is no reason to feel hurt.

647. Don't ever be afraid to say what you feel, but always do it lovingly.

648. Don't get to the point where each spouse knows exactly what the other is going to say and do because by then the mystery is gone, and there are no more surprises.

649. There are five ways to accept honest criticism: to be insulted, to be depressed, to be angry, to ignore it or to be grateful a flaw has been pointed out, and only the last one is useful.

650. Learning to love is somewhat like learning to walk: it requires stumbling and falling many times before mastery is finally attained.

651. You cannot lose once you come to the realization that relationships are all about teaching us how to be more giving and not about receiving.

652. Sexual desire tends to diminish when emotional stresses increase and increase when stress decreases.

653. If you feel that you're giving too much and receiving too little in return, perhaps you don't understand the meaning of love.

654. The power of appreciation is what keeps the enthusiasm alive within a relationship.

655. Forgiveness is "letting go" and "moving on"; it's building a bridge between two lovers by tearing down the wall that separates them.

656. When two people defend the "I'm right, you're wrong" syndrome, it precipitates a long drawn-out power struggle.

657. A relationship will get boring when you fail to pay attention to what attracted you to your mate in the first place.

658. Watch your finances—it's the number one area of conflict between spouses and it works best as a joint venture.

659. It's difficult to forget the malicious things that are said in the heat of an argument; that's why they should never be said!

660. In unhealthy marriages there develops a pecking order, one person who makes most of the demands and another who acquiesces to them.

661. It is a common assumption that couples are responsible for each other's happiness and it falsely relieves us of our own responsibilities.

662. It is by acceptance of each other that two lovers meet each other's needs, not by trying to change one another.

663. You can't share with your mate what you don't own yourself.

664. As long as your inner strength is stronger than outward circumstances, you will remain superior to fate itself.

665. If you honestly view your mate as the most wonderful person in the world, chances are those feelings will be reciprocated.

666. Two people in love can create wondrous things together if neither of them cares who gets the credit for what they do.

667. When you know who you are, when you have your act together, only then can you empower your beloved to get his or her act together.

668. There is a fine line between pleasing your mate and acceding to his or her every demand, simply because the ego can never be satisfied, no matter how accommodating one might try to be.

669. Kindness is the quickest known route to what it is you desire from your beloved.

670. The more you expect from a relationship, the more difficult it is going to be.

671. If you expect your mate to be perfect, you're in for a long, hard winter of a relationship.

672. Whenever you place too many conditions on how your mate should behave, you are potentially setting him or her up to rebel.

673. If you want to remain in your marriage, don't set standards of conduct that are just about impossible for your partner to meet.

674. To do more and more for your mate so he or she has less and less to do is setting yourself up for co-dependency.

675. What your mate might need sometimes is just a sympathetic ear or a shoulder to lean on.

676. Don't expect your mate to be happy just because you solve his or her problems; the mastery of life doesn't work that way. Happiness can only be had by solving your own problems.

677. Don't ever allow your partner's unhappiness to cause you to believe that you are a failure; his or her continued unhappiness is his or her personal problem!

678. Marriages demand quality time together, not necessarily quantity time.

679. Whenever people enter into a relationship with the belief that another person is going to fill their emptiness, there is no way the union can survive.

680. In healthy relationships, people view one another as unique, one-of-a-kind individuals; there is no attempt to control, to be a caretaker, to create dependency.

681. Communication often gets confused by either the need to be right or the need to prove another person wrong.

682. Your mate is the number one person in your life, which is good enough reason not to treat him or her as second-best.

683. Never allow your petty annoyances to turn themselves into serious grudges.

684. Anything nasty you might say during an argument has a way of being remembered long after the squabble, so be careful of what you say to each other.

685. The ground rules of a marriage do not have to remain the same for life, but can and should be renegotiated when needed by either party.

686. Avoid being suspicious about your mate as it has an insidious way of poisoning a relationship.

687. It's not what you get out of a relationship that matters, but what you put into it.

688. Being by yourself is important so try to give your mate as much "space" as he or she requires and expect the same for yourself.

689. When your mate is obviously angry, special pains should be taken not to engage each other in a dialogue because anger only makes one even more unreasonable.

690. Men generally don't like to discuss their problems as much as women do, and understanding this difference is crucial in supporting each other.

691. Don't minimize your mate's problems or invalidate them; what's important for one person may not be important to another

692. Negative comments have a way of keeping another person from communicating back longer than need be.

693. The longer one person tries to invalidate the feelings of another, the longer that person will resist having their feelings invalidated.

694. Angry people almost always believe themselves to be right, even when it is evident how wrong their conduct is; this is why anger can create enormous gaps between two people.

695. By the little word known as "belief," you'll create and live in a heaven or hell of your own making.

696. No storm ever burdens a relationship when a couple believes no storm can harm it.

697. Being honest in your relationship begins by being honest with yourself.

698. Problems are just challenges and opportunities in a marriage for each of you to live up to your best.

699. If your attitude in a relationship is to get the other person to change, the result is generally a good deal of emotional pain and very little change.

700. Everyone has different sexual preferences and needs and they should be intimately shared with one another if you expect to have a satisfying sex life.

701. The more you complain to your mate, the more you open the door for your mate to complain back.

702. Whenever you approach your mate with judgment, the more you require him or her to go on the defensive.

703. Offering your mate unsolicited advice is a "no-no" and only heightens the odds of getting turned off altogether.

704. Blame seldom works in the manner you think it is going to work because it destroys the very cement that binds a relationship together.

705. Every successful human relationship requires daily compromise, and this is especially so of marriage.

706. Early in a relationship both parties generally put their best foot forward; later on the other foot makes itself known and life gets more interesting.

707. Preferences always garner more attention than demands and compliments more than criticism.

708. Whenever a wife mothers her husband or a husband fathers his wife, the marriage is quietly sinking in quicksand.

709. Whenever you find your beloved grumbling, it signals the need for better communication.

710. The secret to getting more from your mate is to make him or her feel appreciated.

711. Good communication is keeping your total attention upon what your mate is saying when he or she is talking to you.

712. No two people ever show their love in exactly the same way; if they did all love would soon be boring.

713. Love is something one grows into, not something one falls into; if you fall in love, you can also fall out of love very easily.

714. To expect your mate to behave according to your expectations destroys his or her uniqueness.

715. True love is doggedly persistent and seldom blossoms in the hearts of those who give up easily.

716. Reduce your expectations; if you always have expectations, whatever you get will never be enough and you'll always expect more.

717. A good mate is someone who will support you and encourage you, but not attempt to rescue you from self-inflicted problems.

718. Take charge of your life; if you don't learn how to take charge and run your personal life, there will always be others who will try to.

719. Set goals together, but be realistic about what you can accomplish within a given time frame.

720. Put the goals of marriage in writing and place them in a conspicuous spot where you can observe them daily.

721. Make up a balanced budget and stick with it "come hell or high water."

722. Frequently visualize your completed marriage goals, together with your beloved and by yourself alone.

723. Good communication is listening intently to what your partner has to say and then not trying to give advice afterward.

724. Just because you understand your mate does not mean you have to be in agreement with him or her.

725. Don't be an "interrupter"; allow your mate to finish his or her communication without correction or criticism.

726. If a relationship is to shine brilliantly, it must first be polished like a diamond and to do this requires some sort of friction.

727. In a marriage you don't just give what you have to the other person, but you give who and what you are!

728. If it's peace you aspire to in your marriage, you need only give up all thought of conflict.

729. Whenever you enter into a serious talk with your beloved always acknowledge first how much he or she means to you before beginning.

730. You gain the love of your mate by being interested in him or her, not by how interesting or uninteresting you are.

731. The entire sum of marriage revolves around the chemistry of one person being genuinely needed by another person, and vice versa.

732. Never underestimate the power of two hearts melded together in the name of God.

733. All love evaporates the moment one heart begins to exercise authority over another heart.

734. The marriage commitments that endure are generally born in the heart; the ones that end up on the scrap heap are generally conceived in the mind.

735. Patience is always the best remedy for every marital problem; impatience, the worst.

736. If you put God first in your relationship, everything else has no choice but to naturally fall into place.

737. In marriage, as in life, nothing worthwhile comes easy.

738. If you find a lot of problems cropping up in your relationship—take a good long look at yourself—the problem is probably the way you are thinking.

739. A giver of love cannot ever be hurt or exploited as long as he or she is not trying to receive something in return.

740. If you want your beloved to grow, it doesn't make sense to do for them what they should be doing for themselves. There is no greater gift you can give than to encourage self-reliance.

741. Never reject offhand what your beloved asks of you without first giving it serious consideration.

742. Life is short—go on as many second, third and fourth honeymoons as you can afford.

743. Insulting remarks, sarcasm and personal affronts are to be avoided if arguments are to be settled rapidly.

744. There are times when it is important to be alone and times when it is important to be together.

745. Don't attempt to impress your mate with how much you know or, for that matter, how little you know.

746. It's easy to be a giver in a relationship because it is the giver who is in control most of the time.

747. What makes good communication so difficult is the "ego" always wanting its own way; eliminate the ego and comunication is virtually assured.

748. Home is not a place to let off steam from the pressures of work, but a refuge from the outside world.

749. As long as it is your desire to possess someone, you lose the capability of giving to or receiving from them.

750. The problem with creating a set of beliefs about your marriage is that when you do so, you begin to set boundaries, and more often than not exclude those things most beneficial to your best interest.

751. As a tree clings to the ground in order to survive, so must a marriage cling to a proper set of principles if it is to thrive.

752. You will receive much more cooperation by speaking *to* your mate, rather than speaking *at* him or her.

753. An all-or-nothing mentality destroys a relationship quicker than anything; what this attitude says is that if something is not great, it's not useful at all.

754. Always remember that whenever you express anger, depression, worry or jealousy, you are actually making a choice to feel that way.

755. Saying exactly what you're feeling doesn't mean dredging up past resentments or negations; it's all about being honest in a positive way.

756. The denial of sex should never be used as a punishment, nor should sex ever be used as a reward.

757. Being married doesn't give you any valid reason to get out of shape or to be less attractive than you were before marriage.

758. Home should be that type of environment that you want to return to after a hard day's work, not to avoid.

759. If there are no problems or challenges in your life together, maybe you should be taking more risks.

760. In the language of love, criticism hurts the heart of both giver and receiver alike.

761. The positive marriage is viewed as a joyful learning experience; the negative, as a life sentence in prison.

762. Put resentment into your relationship and create hell for yourself; replace it with love and your life will become heaven.

763. Never dredge up old issues in a current dispute.

764. In all discussions, be concerned that you first understand before you are understood.

765. If your actions don't match up with your words, you're being a hypocrite.

766. If you feel guilty saying "no," you're not in charge of your life.

767. Never give your mate an ultimatum lest you be the loser in the long run.

768. Find out what particular interests your spouse delights in and try to become at least conversant in them.

769. Flirting with your spouse doesn't end after the honeymoon, but should continue for the duration of the relationship.

770. Sexual expectations sometimes have to be negotiated just as every other part of a relationship has to be negotiated.

771. The excitement of getting to know each other does not last forever, but will eventually evolve into a more mature excitement of growing up together.

772. When your mate is melancholy it's not your duty to jump into the swamps of depression with him or her, but to do whatever you can to lift him or her out.

773. Whatever insecurities you bring into a marriage have a way of magnifying themselves, sometimes out of control.

774. When the honeymoon is over, every marriage begins in earnest, and every honeymoon does have an end!

775. You can tell how healthy your marriage is by the way you fight; if you are disrespectful or abusive to your spouse, your relationship can hardly be called healthy.

776. The secret of every successful relationship is for each of you to love doing what you are doing.

777. If you make your marriage the first priority in life, it will serve as a springboard for everything else.

778. It is always wiser to convince your mate with a plea to the heart than an appeal to the head.

779. Whenever you want to discuss something important, go to where the two of you can be alone together without interruption.

780. Regarding sex, if you reject your mate often enough you will paralyze him or her from ever taking the initiative.

781. Variety is the spice of life, so treat each other to places and things you've never seen or done before.

782. Being your upbeat, positive self beats the falsity of trying to be "clever" or "charming."

783. If you can't take the time to be with your spouse because of business, you don't control the business, the business controls you.

784. Whenever either of you is unable to fill the other person's needs, then there is a need to negotiate a compromise.

785. Every once in a while take inventory of the basic qualities of the other that brought you together in the first place.

786. Your beloved is the most essential thing in your life, so don't waste your time on unessential things.

787. If you neglect to listen to the demands of your body, your body will eventually neglect to listen to you.

788. Your spiritual health should take first priority in your life followed by your mental, physical and financial health.

789. Learn to give one another foot and body massages.

790. If you smoke or drink, you are not only doing your body a disservice, but you are placing an unfair burden on your mate as well.

791. Establish an exercise routine together with your mate and encourage each other to keep up with it.

792. Don't allow old, bad habits to keep you from making new choices in your life.

793. It serves no useful purpose to talk about old loves, so keep your mouth shut on this matter.

794. People who do not know how to say "no" to family and friends invariably spread themselves too thin in their marriage.

795. Surprise your mate with a mystery ride or a mystery date or even a mystery vacation, just the two of you together.

796. Be more spontaneous; it breaks the mold we call "conformity" and makes for more excitement in a marriage.

797. Never pass up a reason to celebrate a "success" together.

798. Maturity is accepting the things in your relationship you can't change and changing the things you can.

799. Nothing pleases your mate more than knowing that you want to please him or her more than anything else in the world.

800. If you don't learn how to forgive and let go, you'll end up carrying a large bag of resentment the rest of your life.

801. The more grateful you are of your mate, the more he or she will sense it and try to make you even more grateful.

802. If you listen more and say less, half the problems in a relationship will be eliminated.

803. Contrary to popular opinion all sexual excitement originates in the mind; where there is no sexual stimulation in the mind, there is no sex.

804. Never do anything that would damage the self-esteem of your beloved. A low self-esteem not only undermines him or her, but your entire marriage as well.

805. Whenever you lean on a relationship to supply your own happiness, you set up a mechanism to cause it to crumble.

806. Many people believe alcohol is an aphrodisiac because it lowers inhibitions, but in truth it is a depressant that, with prolonged use, reduces sexual desire.

807. What a marriage does best is expose the weaknesses of each other.

808. Don't mentally make comparisons of your mate with lovers from the past.

809. It's never to late to apologize, to admit you are wrong, to begin anew.

810. Praising your mate before marriage is a matter of preference, but praising your mate afterwards is a matter of necessity.

811. Love tends to change over the years from youthful passion to devotion, loyalty and companionship. Enjoy the seasons of life.

812. Don't spend too much time trying to figure out your beloved, just concentrate on loving him or her.

813. Don't give in to the temptation to rescue your spouse every time he or she has a personal problem.

814. Men generally define themselves by their work and accomplishments, women by their children and their relationships, so support each other the best way you can.

815. Assertiveness in a relationship is not a tool to get your way but a valuable way of standing up for your own rights.

816. Good communication in marriage is what breath is to life—there is nothing more vital.

817. The use of anger has few, if any, positive results and the less it occurs the healthier and happier a marriage will be.

818. You don't help your mate by doing more for them than they can do for themselves.

819. Ultimately, there is no such thing as controlling the actions of someone else; there is only controlling yourself.

820. You can't love unconditionally until you give up the idea you "need" to be loved in return.

821. Don't be afraid to communicate with your partner about sex, what you like, as well as what you don't like.

822. Marriage, for most of those participating in it, is a continuous process of getting used to things you least expect.

823. Whenever you are fixated upon one solution to a marital problem, it keeps you from finding the less-obvious alternatives.

824. We do not love our beloved because they are beautiful, but they appear beautiful because we love them.

825. Just as you cannot withdraw money from a bank without first making a deposit, neither can you receive love without first giving it out.

826. What commitment means is that you will do everything possible to make a relationship work.

827. As a general rule, the more open and honest a relationship is, the stronger it becomes.

828. Marriage should make you feel better about yourself, not worse; if you are feeling worse, something is wrong with your relationship.

829. The surest way to mess up a relationship is to practice the three C's: Complaining, Criticizing, and Condemning.

830. Never waste an opportunity to tell your beloved how much he or she means to you.

831. Women operate on emotional truth, men on logical truth; and here the difference between the sexes lies.

832. Love is the most misused word and for most people it is mistaken for sex, but sex is not love nor is love sex.

833. Whenever selfishness is removed from a relationship, there is no desire to get anything from your beloved.

834. How can you tell if love is genuine? True love does not change, and if you find it changing, it never was love to begin with.

835. The intimacy of marriage has a way of stripping off the masks, if any, worn during courtship.

836. Your most important relationship is with yourself; most people form relationships to avoid themselves.

837. Principles are like a compass: if you both adhere to the same principles, you'll never get lost, you'll always know the way.

838. If a relationship has a _why_ behind it, a satisfactory meaning for its existence, it can deal with any _what_ or _where_.

839. You can't have a quality relationship unless you invest the time; what you put into a relationship is exactly what you get out of it.

840. Shortcuts do not work in marriage; the law of cause and effect will always apply, no matter how hard one tries to "beat the system."

841. Successful couples manage their time together around rock-solid principles; the unsuccessful, around tasks, duties and obligations.

842. Every person needs his or her own private space and every relationship must set up guidelines to maintain that space.

843. Do not expect marriage to bring you peace; inner peace is within—it is an internal affair. It cannot be found by sleeping next to someone else, no matter how pleasurable that may be.

844. The communication level in a marriage has a way of deteriorating whenever the level of trust begins to run low.

845. The longer it takes for two people to face up to a problem within a relationship, the greater the problem becomes.

846. Within the heart of every person is a deep longing to be valued and appreciated; ignore these needs within your mate and be prepared for an unsettling marriage.

847. People hold on to their pain and suffering because they have made a choice to hold on; the same choice can be made for joy and happiness if they choose to.

848. If angry people knew they were being imprisoned by their own anger, there would be very little outrage between two people.

849. Coercion does not strengthen a marriage, but weakens it; you do not make a marriage stronger by making threats to leave it.

850. The private, personal victories of your mate occur when he or she gains self-esteem; the defeats, when esteem is lost.

851. The difference between men and women is that one wants sex and the other romance; one looks to relieve tension by sex and the other to gradually build up the sexual tension.

852. If you take the time to look hard enough, whatever you look for in a mate, you will find it.

853. Keeping a marriage intact over the long haul requires more than wishful thinking; it demands the commitment and willpower to overcome all obstacles.

854. If your mate does something unwittingly to offend you, it becomes your responsibility to politely call attention to that matter.

855. When a relationship becomes strained, extreme care must be given to the quality and content of our words lest they produce even more strain.

856. Differences of opinion don't necessarily weaken a marriage; sometimes they add another dimension to it and make it even stronger.

857. The act of patience is the highest form of love and sometimes there is no need to say anything because patience itself can speak louder than words.

858. From time to time, get together with your beloved and write down all the things you have in common; this will give you both an opportunity to reminisce together.

859. The only control worth having in a relationship is self-control not control over our beloved.

860. When two people disagree it doesn't mean one is right and one is wrong; it simply means they see things differently.

861. There can be no successful marriage without sacrifice, because it always requires some sort of surrender to service the needs of two or more people.

862. A relationship can only be built by trust and trust can only result from trusting.

863. To yell and scream in order to get your point across is communication at the lowest level—it does nothing to build a closer relationship.

864. Compromise works best early in a disagreement, seldom as a last resort.

865. Be persistent; everything isn't going to be your way all the time—that's not how life operates.

866. Communication, compromise and commitment are the three essentials to every happy marriage.

867. Even when you're not happy with a proposed compromise—accept it anyway and get on with life.

868. Complainers have a way of repeating the words "always" and "never" over and over again; don't be a complainer!

869. When a relationship is fragile, words are often misinterpreted; when it is strong, there is almost no need for words.

870. Set realistic goals for your marriage; it's difficult to hit a target that both of you cannot envision.

871. Trying to organize your life with the specific intention of making your mate happy is an effort doomed to failure; you can only make yourself happy.

872. Happiness is everyone's birthright—know it belongs to you and it cannot be given to or taken away by anyone else.

873. Every couple decides what is acceptable and what is not acceptable in their marriage and this trial-and-error process may require years before it is complete. You just have to faithfully hang in there!

874. If only you would dare to believe it—the universe is always conspiring only to do you good, even if it might seem otherwise.

875. Don't neglect to love yourself; the more you love yourself, the more you are able to love your beloved.

876. You cannot discover new horizons together unless you both muster up the courage to deliberately lose sight of the shore together.

877. Your attitude determines your attitude; it is the first indication of the kind of person you are within, so always try to maintain a cheerful attitude.

878. Every successful marriage has a safe environment where disagreements are sanely discussed, a place where there is no risk to the relationship itself.

879. Be wary of giving constructive criticism because, more often than not, it can be perceived as tearing the other person down.

880. The measure of how well your relationship is doing is laughter; if it's doing well—there is a lot to laugh about together.

881. Some of your needs can only be filled by you and some by others—and wisdom is knowing the difference between the two.

882. No person can share completely with another person; there are always parts of us we must discover for ourselves.

883. A relationship is a living thing requiring constant attention and if left unattended, it will die by atrophy!

884. All habits are learned, hence all bad habits can be unlearned if the aspiration is great enough to undo them.

885. The first prerequisite for change is that a person must really want to change.

886. The successful marriage has a clear idea of what the participants desire; the unsuccessful ones are not quite sure.

887. Your outer world is a reflection of your inner world; what is happening without is largely a matter of what is quietly happening within.

888. There is nothing more that you can ask from a marriage then to live well, laugh often and love much.

889. A marriage that does not protect the rights of the parties within the marriage is hardly worth saving.

890. Encouraging your beloved to grow, to stretch out his or her wings and fly, does not mean he or she is going to fly away, but is a means to bring you closer together.

891. When one person demands that another change or demands that there be no change, there is little understanding of the meaning of unconditional love.

892. The worst encroachment you can commit against your mate is not to let him or her be himself or herself.

893. A relationship should bring more comfort than discomfort; if it is bringing more discomfort than comfort, let it be a wake-up call to change.

894. A marriage with well-defined goals will make progress toward that goal no matter how difficult the road may be.

895. Never demolish dreams; never make a decision that will compromise the heart's desire of your beloved.

896. Anyone who goes into a marriage and says, "I'll change him or her after we are married" is also deluding himself or herself.

897. Romance has a way of blocking out reality; marriage, a way of bringing it back.

898. There rarely ever has been a successful union of souls that was not first preceded by a series of failures that had to be overcome.

899. Marriages frequently run into difficulty when a husband or wife is unable to separate from his or her original family. Here a fine balance must be kept.

900. We-ness gives a marriage staying power to put up with the frustrations of life; where I-ness replaces we-ness, difficulties are inevitable.

901. Some couples need to find more time together, some less; each couple must decide the measure of time together that is right for them.

902. Marriage is all about sharing, yielding and giving up freedoms and those who enter into matrimony with desires other than this are only deluding themselves.

903. It's not necessary for couples to share equally in a crisis, rather each should do what he or she can at the time.

904. A marriage doesn't just happen; it requires a great deal of time sorting things out together. That's why patience is such an important commodity.

905. Compromise is all about meeting your partner halfway, and sometimes this means accepting only a portion of the pie instead of the whole.

906. Children have a way of either weakening or strengthening a marital bond; rarely does a marriage remain the same after the birth of a child.

907. If you are going to spend the rest of your life with someone, it better be a person you can be comfortable with first and attracted to second.

908. Marriages are consummated on two levels, the physical and the mental. The former is done on the wedding night, the latter can take quite a few years to accomplish.

909. You are always in control of a relationship as long as you don't want anything from your beloved; once something is wanted, you are being controlled by your wants.

910. Making your mate feel guilty in order to get what you want is a despicable game; don't play it, don't allow it to be played on you.

911. If your mate tries to place a guilt trip on you, simply inquire of him or her, "Are you asking me to feel guilty?"

912. Forgiveness means you pardon your mate for everything; you can't pick and choose what you will forgive and what you will not forgive.

913. Unresolved anger and unsettled grudges prevent a marriage from ever escaping the quicksand of unhappiness.

914. Everyone makes silly, stupid mistakes, but the hallmark of a mature couple is that they are never regretful or remorseful over them.

915. Scratch your mate's back, give him or her a foot or body massage and you'll find a permanent job for life.

916. What makes a relationship work is consistency and without consistency there is a tendency toward pain.

917. What the intimacy of marriage does is expose the beautiful, as well as the ugly, like no other spotlight can.

918. Don't become so obsessed in your parenting as to forget your relationship with your partner; he or she will be around long after the kids are gone.

919. Marriage is not easy, it requires continuous hard work; harmony does not just happen, it requires ceaseless negotiation.

920. Balancing the needs of your spouse along with those of your children is probably the most difficult job within a marriage.

921. If a marriage is given priority over parenting and maintains eminence over the workplace, it is in very little danger of collapsing.

922. Crises have a way of galvanizing two people together or shearing them apart; they will either make or break a relationship.

923. Coping with a tantrum is largely a matter of informing your mate you are not going to discuss things until his or her behavior changes.

924. Marriage is not a panacea for getting what you want; even in the greatest of unions there are desires, wants and needs that must remain unfulfilled.

925. What marriage is all about is transformation, two incomplete people coming together in an attempt to become complete, but in truth marriage can not make you complete because you are complete already.

926. Trying to change your mate is like trying to change the world; it would be more effective to change your view of your mate or of the world.

927. Don't make demands; to make demands in the name of the relationship is weakening the union, not strengthening it.

928. Tidiness comes next to cleanliness so have a place for everything and put all things back in their proper place.

929. Confidentiality is important; when one person cannot confide their innermost thoughts without fear of ridicule, a breakdown in the union is forthcoming.

930. Women partake of sex to receive love, men love to partake in sex, and this play between the sexes is what keeps the dance between the male and female alive.

931. If you can't reach your mate with kind, endearing words of love, it's useless to attempt to communicate any other way.

932. When one spouse says to the other, "You must be the way I want you to be," he or she is placing an unreasonable demand upon the relationship.

933. Be respectful of little things; a lot of petty annoyances place as much strain on a marriage as one large problem.

934. Each person should respect the right to privacy of the other; everyone needs time to be alone without the other person feeling threatened by it.

935. When one person makes most of the demands in a relationship and another fulfills them, the former has become a malcontent and the latter is his or her co-dependent.

936. The only way a marriage can function on all cylinders is between equals.

937. Everyone has secrets and it's O.K. not to share an inner thought until one can comfortably find words to express it adequately.

938. A certain amount of freedom is essential for every relationship because without some sort of autonomy one or both of the participants begins to feel trapped and longs to be free.

939. Nobody can defend your personal rights except you, and if you don't protect them, no one else will!

940. Gratitude does not stop because you are married; "Thank you" are two words that can never be overused.

941. Marriage does not automatically bestow the right of guardianship or caretakership upon one over the other.

942. Hiding problems in hopes they'll go away is more destructive than bringing them to the forefront and openly discussing them.

943. A marriage not committed to hanging in there during the ups and downs of growing together cannot be counted upon to stay together.

944. Sex without the deepest feelings for the other person is nothing more than a mechanical act.

945. If a marriage is going to be successful, both parties *must* maintain their separate identities; when boundaries merge, difficulties ensue.

946. When a marriage is going well there is a ripple effect that extends to other areas of one's life; and the same is true when things are not going well.

947. Only you can make you feel complete and to expect your mate to complete you is making an unreasonable demand that cannot be satisfied.

948. Relationships would be easy if feelings didn't fluctuate, but they do, and that's what often makes communication difficult.

949. The only words worth speaking are those from the heart; better to remain silent than talk about what's on your mind, because generally the mind can be very fickle.

950. When one person listens to another without interruption, both are practicing communication at the highest level.

951. There are no hard and fast rules to keep two people together, but every successful relationship makes up a set to guide them along the way.

952. People who have truly learned how to love _never_ feel cheated that they haven't gotten back what they justly desire; giving for them is award enough.

953. Happiness is your original nature and if you are not happy with yourself, you can't blame your unhappiness on someone else.

954. Everything that is visible between two hearts is sustained by the invisible; until this is actually realized there will always be a grasping for greater meaning to life.

955. Loving is really caring about the other person's feelings just as much as you care about your own.

956. A relationship that does not have a specific goal will have trouble getting back on track after being derailed by a crisis.

957. The only thing harder than expressing your feelings is understanding the feelings of another person.

958. Never doubt that life is one indivisible whole and how ethically or unethically you operate in one area of life will ultimately affect your marriage as well.

959. Intimacy is difficult to define between two people because what is intimate for one person can be an invasion of privacy for another.

960. You have no right to expect your mate to clean up after you.

961. Growth in one area of your relationship is a precursor of growth in other areas of your life as well.

962. A marriage is an agreement between two people to live together and to be valid it must allow for growth on both sides.

963. Marriage is all about creating a "safe space" together in what is often a hostile world.

964. The dynamics of a relationship are forever changing; whatever might have been true last month is not necessarily true today.

965. The secret to venting your feelings is to *never* speak unfavorably or unkindly about your partner.

966. A good sense of humor has a way of keeping problems in their proper perspective.

967. Take precious time to be together; children and work can often take up so much of your time there is hardly any left for a relationship.

968. Listen to what your beloved is trying to say; the most difficult problem in marital communication is that many couples only hear what they want to hear.

969. Two people who are continually supporting and nurturing each other cannot help but grow closer in the process.

970. What most marriages thrive on is rock-solid commitment; you don't keep a candle burning by continually threatening to blow it out.

971. Personal freedom allows your lover to grow by not distracting him or her with your demands on how he or she should act.

972. Try to save a part of your monthly income for a "rainy day."

973. The happiest marriage is one that continually focuses on what it does have—not on what it doesn't.

974. You learn to keep romance alive in a relationship simply by never taking your beloved for granted.

975. Men are sexually aroused visually; women are sexually aroused verbally; now that you have been made aware of this truth, try to take advantage of it.

976. A husband does not possess his wife nor does a wife possess her husband and as long as attempts to possess occur, friction is the inevitable result.

977. You don't have to have sex if you don't feel like it, but you do owe your lover a reasonable explanation.

978. The vow two lovers take during their wedding does not end courtship; courtship should continue until death dissolves the union.

979. One of the fallacies regarding marriage is that two lovers should attempt to become one, but when this occurs in practice the end result is two half-people.

980. Marriage is much easier on your relationship when families are begun after you are financially and emotionally secure.

981. If you don't live within your means, you risk your marriage being shipwrecked on the shoals of financial excess.

982. Those people who do not know how to forgive and forget are destined for much pain and suffering in their marriages.

983. One difference between men and women is that generally men use sex to gain intimacy while women require intimacy prior to sex.

984. Mature couples never, ever have offspring simply as a means to keep their relationship intact.

985. Sex without love to give it value is an empty experience.

986. Until you learn to love your Self there will always be a limitation on your love for others.

987. Be natural; be who you are; whenever you try to make an impression on your mate, all you are doing is validating your own insecurity.

988. Marriage is a classroom where you are being taught to give to your beloved, and to keep on giving, without counting the cost.

989. Don't underestimate the value of sending flowers to your beloved for no special reason at all.

990. Love only exists in the present moment—past love is of little value nor is future love; love to be love must always be now.

991. A couple only thinking about each other's happiness will soon find themselves rich in a storehouse of happiness.

992. It's up to each of you to discover what turns your partner on and to shy away from what turns your partner off.

993. Thinking only about yourself is what turns your lover off more than anything else.

994. Communicate your sexual needs; sex is one of the most common complaints in marriage, falling into two categories: too much and not enough.

995. You can practice all the sexual techniques in the world but without the feeling of love to accompany them, they are of little value.

996. Too much "togetherness" does not always make for a healthy relationship; sometimes a time apart is needed as a way of energizing your marriage.

997. The success or failure of a relationship is ultimately determined by how your beloved feels in your presence; if his or her self-esteem is being enhanced, that is a positive sign; if the reverse if true, there are going to be rough times.

998. Just because a relationship is hurting doesn't mean you have to be hurting; happiness is a state of mind, not the state of a relationship at a given time.

999. Foreplay and afterplay are just as important in a relationship, if not more so, than the sexual act itself.

1000. Marriages work best when each person is more than willing to give sixty percent and have no qualms about receiving only forty percent.

1001. Marriage gives the opportunity to learn one of the most important lessons of life, unconditional love: to give to your beloved and to your children, and to keep on giving, without counting the cost.

1002. Help is not telling your beloved what to do, it's just being there to lend support, to offer encouragment and share in his or her experience.

1003. Whether you realize it or not, problems help marriages to grow; where there are problems, personal growth is not too far behind.

1004. If your heart doesn't know who it is, there will always be a piece missing when two hearts attempt to come together as one.

1005. Love is a most difficult word to define because for most people the definition changes over the years.

1006. The greatest challenge with relationships is not blurring the boundaries that determine who we really are.

1007. Keep this book at your bedside and go over one truth at a time every night for a thousand and eight nights; and when you're done, start over.

1008. Every marriage should come with an instruction manual, but since there is none, this book is the closest you'll get to one.

☿

The Final Message
of Athena:

MY DEAR PRINCE, MY DEAR
PRINCESS: the time grows short,
soon both of you will return to the
womb and be born into humanness.
Everything has been prepared for you.
Your parents have been selected, as well
as an auspicious meeting in the future.
You need not fear that you will not
remember each other; non-recognition
is virtually impossible. From the very
first moment you lay eyes upon one
another, there will be an immediate
sense of *deja vu*. It will seem as if you
have known each other for countless
lifetimes, and of course, this is true.

You will not be able to shake the
feeling of familiarity. There will be a

feeling of comfortableness, like two old shoes coming together to make a complete pair. An inner voice will quietly confirm what each of you already know—you have been brought together to learn the lessons of marriage.

But I must digress here and warn you that the density of the earthly plane is going to play silly tricks with the mind. At the beginning of your relationship, you are both going to believe that, by coming together in a physical way, you have become whole and complete as individuals. But this is far from the truth, my dear Andrew and Cheryl.

Wholeness or completeness cannot be found simply by being in close proximity to another person, nor can it be transferred from one to another. The door to completeness must be unlocked from within. No one can make us whole if we do not maintain a wholeness within ourselves; two half-people cannot come together and magically transform themselves overnight. Two half-people will always remain fractions until they take the time and make the effort to make themselves whole.

What marriage does is act as a catalyst to bring us closer to wholeness, but it is not an end in itself. Relationships are more like a school where lessons are presented and tests are provided to see if the participants have mastered their lessons. Happiness is proof that one has received a passing grade; pain and suffering mean more improvement is required.

The mistake each of you made during your last incarnation was believing that two people coming together in matrimony constituted some sort of a final wholeness. You thought you could lay down the oars to your "Love Boat" and float down the river of life undisturbed. You were deceived by the early euphoria of getting to know each other, and when that feeling eventually wore off, your relationship fell apart. A successful marriage requires diligence and work—lots of hard work. Anyone who tells you otherwise either does not know or is deceiving you.

What marriage is is a series of choices to be loving or unloving to your beloved. The ultimate decision is always yours. If you are loving, I can guarantee that happiness will stalk you like an unshakable shadow; but should either of you choose to be unloving, I can also guarantee unhappiness will follow doggedly in your footsteps. Heaven and hell are states of mind and both are only one thought away. Heaven is reserved for the loving; hell, for the unloving. Be attentive to my words; it is not uncommon on the material plane for two people to be living under the same roof, the thoughts of one can be in heaven and the thoughts of the other struggling in hell.

The scales of a marriage must be

delicately balanced with giving and receiving. But also know that you will only get out of the relationship what you are first willing to put into it and not one iota more. If you wisely put more in than you take out, you will partake of a blessing of joy, but if you attempt to take out more than what you are willing to put in, the scales will act as if they had been defrauded. It is foolishness indeed to expect more for less, and one will be required to pay a heavy price for such a transgression. Know that it is mandatory that one first give in a relationship before receiving anything in return; and also know that there is little happiness gained from receiving when it is compared to giving.

Listen carefully to my words, my dear prince, my dear princess, because marriage is the coming together of equals. And if there is no equality within your giving and receiving, it becomes an unbalanced affair. Love is nothing more than giving, giving, giving, without the thought of receiving anything in return. And it is the absence of giving that places a strain on marriages. Two people giving sixty percent and satisfied with receiving only forty percent back is the ideal. Nothing more is asked of you. But it is also enough to make all the angels in heaven sing at such an event.

Take heed, my dear prince and princess, that neither of you falls into the trap of taking more out of the marriage than you are willing to put back into it. It is not possible to enter into a relationship with the idea that another person is going to fill your void and creatively color your emptiness. To expect this is simply immaturity. It is not going to happen. Only you can make yourself happy, no one else. And if you expect your relationship to thrive, you had better not be depending on someone else to fill those gaps that only you can possibly fill.

Know that the first prerequisite to becoming the ideal lover is to love yourself. If you want to be loved, you must first make yourself lovable. And if you can't love yourself, neither should you expect to be able to love your beloved.

Do you understand what I am trying to tell you, Andrew? No one has the right to ask, "What am I getting out of my marriage?" without honestly first answering the question, "How much am I putting into my marriage?" The law is explicit. We only receive back what we are willing to give out. And we cannot give too much without discovering that we cannot give something out without somehow receiving an equal measure back. Do you desire love? Be loving! Do you long for peace? Be peaceful! Do you desire joy? Be joyful.

Do you fathom what I am trying to reveal to you, Cheryl? The center of your heart must be one of giving. Know that there is no such thing as giving too much of yourself. It is up to you to find a way to give the best you know how, and whatever that best is cannot but fly back to you. And this is only the beginning; when the art of freely giving without expectations is mastered, the very heavens will open to shower you with blessings.

During our dialogue together, I have revealed one thousand and eight secrets of a happy marriage, but know that giving simply for the sake of giving is the greatest secret, towering above all the others. Nothing else can bring marital happiness the way giving without conditions or expectations does. Never doubt for a moment that the only worthwhile love is one that gives without expecting anything in return.

My dear prince and princess: our meeting together must come to an end. Anyone demonstrating the unconditional love of which I speak has crossed over the ocean of selfishness and generally is in no further need of earthly schooling. His or her round of births and deaths comes to an end. I have high hopes your earthly sojourn will not only be a fruitful one, but your final one as well.

What I have told you is the absolute truth and only the foolish would dare to dispute it. Go now in peace and may the spirit of Awareness remain with you until your return Home. ❖

A Radiant Life Series Book:

Cupid's Guidebook
for the Serious Lover
By Andy Zubko
$5.95
This is the first volume in the Prince Andrew and
Princess Cheryl series. The Prince and Princess visit
Cupid who provides them with a foundation of core
values for a successful relationship, in the form of
707 powerful, inspirational and wise insights about
unconditional love. After reading it and placing the
principles into action, your love life will never be the
same again. Excellent gift for your significant other
on Valentine's Day or at any other time of the year.

A RADIANT LIFE SERIES BOOK:

The Wisdom of James Allen
5 Classic Works Combined Into One
By James Allen, edited by Andy Zubko
$7.95

This mysterious Englishman who lived at the turn of the century is best known to the American public as the author of the widely acclaimed spiritual classic, *As a Man Thinketh*. *As a Man Thinketh* is included in this volume, as are four lesser known works, the "lost books" of James Allen. The deep insights of this "mystic" are immensely inspirational in meeting life's challenges. This book is destined to be a classic in itself.

A Radiant Life Series Book:

Let's Get to Know Each Other
By Andy Zubko
$4.95

This is actually more of a delightful process then a book. *Let's Get to Know Each Other* is designed as a fun way for two people to do just that—to get to know each other better by revealing likes and dislikes, strengths and weaknesses, opinions and prejudices, as well as hopes and dreams. It contains a series of three hundred questions, some playful and some involving core values. Each of you fills out the questionnaire and the reward is gettting to know the other on many and deeper levels. Plus, it is a lot of fun when the two of you get together to compare answers.

These books are available at fine book-
stores and other outlets across the country.
If you are not able to obtain a particular
title from your local book store, you may
order it directly from Blue Dove Press
Please add $1.50 for the first book and 50
cents for each additional book for shipping
and handling. Discounts on bulk orders.

Contact: Blue Dove Press
            P. O. Box 261611
            San Diego, CA 92196
            phone: 619–271–0490